LIFE'S 7
PERFECT
COACHES

Winning Habits for
Work, Learning, Leadership, and Life

V. DOUGLAS HINES, PH.D.

About the Cover
The image of a perfect sphere suspended above its reflection symbolizes how
continuous growth requires self-reflection.

Contents

Part Three: Feedback

Skillsets and Habits:
https://users.perfectcoaches.com/home/how_do_i_change

Meet AMI, the computer-based virtual coach:
https://www.youtube.com/watch?v=NoBzkz0G5EU

Habit is thus the enormous fly-wheel of society, its most precious conservative agent. . .

It dooms us all to fight out the battle of life upon the lines of our nurture or our early choice, and to make the best of a pursuit that disagrees, because there is no other for which we are fitted, and it is too late to begin again. . .

The great thing, then, in all education, is to make our nervous system our ally instead of our enemy. It is to fund and capitalize our acquisitions and live at ease upon the interest of the fund. For this we must make automatic and habitual, as early as possible, as many useful actions as we can, and guard against the growing into ways that are likely to be disadvantageous to us, as we should guard against the plague.

William James, *The Principles of Psychology*, 1890. Chapter 4. Habit.

Chapter One
Questions, Answers, Action

Welcome to PerfectCoaches. You are about to discover how self-awareness, and the mindfulness it creates, enhances the quality of what we do and how we experience life.

Self-awareness is a gift every person can enjoy. Just as importantly, it fosters an honesty and clarity of purpose that can improve group life. In that sense, self-awareness is, perhaps, not just a gift, but a responsibly. This concept has been around for centuries, as can be seen in *Hamlet,* when Polonius gives Laertes advice before his son sets out into the world:

> *This above all: to thine own self be true,*
> *And it must follow, as the night the day,*
> *Thou canst not then be false to any man.*

Shakespeare's prose is perfect—if you are true to yourself, you are more likely to be true to others. So many of us know this concept but struggle to find out who we are. PerfectCoaches is designed to help you discover a fuller, deeper self and then use that self-awareness to maximize your life.

PerfectCoaches is for You

The image of a perfect sphere suspended above its reflection is the symbol of PerfectCoaches. It represents how continuous growth requires self-reflection. The Greek philosopher Socrates expressed the importance of this self-awareness in a simple admonition: *Know thyself.* But how, exactly, is this accomplished? He also offered a method, the Socratic dialog, for seeking truth and insight by continuously asking questions. The power of a Socratic dialog derives from the insight contained in both the questions and answers. Asking the right questions in a disciplined way helps you seize each moment and live it, instead of only reacting to it.

Questions, no matter how useful, are abstractions. It is difficult to draw a picture of a question in your mind. Drawing a picture of a person is easier. PerfectCoaches is a *thought experiment* that poses seven fundamental questions about life and invites you to imagine coaches asking the questions. Further, you are invited to draw a mental picture of *perfect coaches:* perfectly patient, disciplined, and accepting every person using the method.

PerfectCoaches is a state-of-the-art package involving *people, process,* and *technology.* The *people* in your work teams receive emphasis. Friends, family, colleagues, and members of other organizations are important, too. You may also have a coach or mentor. People you interact with can provide examples of habits you might want to learn. When you connect with other people, they can also help to reinforce new skills and habits.

The *process* described in this book is a continuous cycle with three key elements: *self-awareness, behavioral focus,* and *feedback.* Self-awareness sets the stage for understanding who you are today while envisioning who you could be tomorrow. Behavioral focus keeps you constantly mindful of the habits you want to master. Feedback sustains focus, increases self-awareness, and keeps the cycle of positive change moving forward.

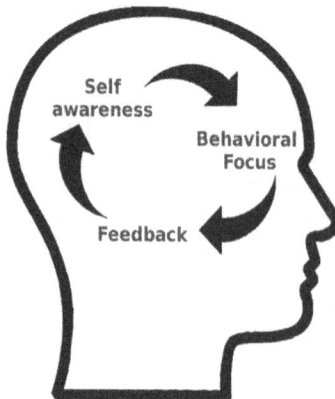

The PerfectCoaches app provides the *technology*. This tool, to be discussed in depth at the end of the book, is not simply a companion piece for the book, it uses a patented 21st century invention to help you achieve the elusive goal, as old as civilization itself— knowing who you are and becoming the person you want to be. The app contains learning modules for the foundational best-practice habits, and a journal enabling you to interact with a virtual coach. The virtual coach can be a person, or it can be AMI, a computer- based helper, whose name stands for Adaptive Motivational Interaction.

The book has nine chapters. Following this introduction, the first chapters describe the PerfectCoaches process.

Self-Awareness

Chapters Two and Three pose the questions which, when answered by you, heighten self-awareness. They are a quick "snapshot" defining *who* you are today, *what* you do now, *why* you do it, and *when* you do it best. In Business Process Reengineering (BPR), a discipline rich in ideas adapted for PerfectCoaches, this could be called your *As-Is* self. Next, attention shifts to your *To-Be* self: *where* you want to go and *how* you get there.

Just thinking about these questions is valuable. Writing the answers down is even better. You can use the Pen and Paper Workbook in this book or, better yet, use the PerfectCoaches app. The apps are available for both iPhone and Android and a web-based version can be found at PerfectCoaches.com.

Behavioral Focus

The self-awareness snapshot helps you identify things you might want to change. The choice of what and how to change is yours. Chapters Three and Four give examples of *best-practice* habits, foundational skills you may want to master. These best practices are not prescribed (i.e.: you must do *this* and do it *this way*). Rather, they represent a curated list of suggestions that have worked well for other people and organizations. The habits are organized into skillsets, a set of related skills that are learned separately but eventually practiced together to achieve a goal. The book presents each of the four main skillsets somewhat differently, reflecting ideas about how they can be used most effectively.

Chapters Four describes habits that foster personal excellence. Although these foundational habits and skills apply to everything you do, every day, they are especially useful for professionals doing "knowledge work" where information and data are compiled and used. Students (apprentice professionals) are another intended audience. The habits students acquire for studying and learning bring success throughout their career. Similarly, although the customer relations skills described in Chapter Five are most relevant in the workplace, they also equip you to deal effectively with others in every context.

In Chapters Six and Seven, attention turns to best-practice habits that pertain to wellness and living life to the fullest. These foundational skills are for everyone, regardless of their occupation or stage of life. PerfectCoaches invites you to imagine what it would be like if you did the best you could do and felt the best you could feel. Achieving that goal involves being thankful for what you have: your powerful human brain, your breath, your body, the people around you—your life itself. Awareness of these gifts paves the way to living each moment mindfully and holistically.

Feedback

Chapter Eight shows you how feedback sustains progress. The conversation with your virtual coach and your PerfectCoaches journal sustains behavioral focus when it provides feedback from a virtual coach in a modern "tweet- like" version of the Socratic dialog. The virtual coach helps you understand the cues that can trigger your behavior and consequences that follow your actions. Being mindful of these cues and consequences helps you master useful habits.

The discussion of feedback within work teams draws on the PerfectCoaches *doctrine of the Four Ts*. People usually get more done in *Teams*—that's the first T—and teams are more successful when team members and leaders *Talk* about goals, *Train* as needed, and *Thank* each other with recognition and awards, both monetary and non-monetary.

Imagining an "inner accountant" asking why you do things, an "inner craftsman" asking when you do them best, and an "inner planner" asking where you are going makes self-discovery interesting. PerfectCoaches also sets the stage for "advanced thought experiments"—dialogs with great ideas and the people, real or fictional, who embody them.

Chapter Nine concludes with an in-depth discussion of the PerfectCoaches thought experiment in which you imagine a conversation with individuals—people you have known, great leaders and thinkers, celebrities, even fictional characters—who serve as models for winning habits, particularly in leadership.

Application to Leadership, Sales, and Customer Service

PerfectCoaches is not just for you, it is also for the groups of every size you interact with every day. Entire organizations and their leaders can use the tools that PerfectCoaches offers.

The chapters on customer relations and leadership focus on one set of work skills, those involving influencing the thoughts and actions of others. It presents a complete, easy-to-master approach to persuasion in sales, leadership, and customer service. Experienced pros and beginners alike can commit the *Ten-Habit Method*™ to memory. Unlike earlier chapters emphasizing best practices cited by other writers, this chapter offers an end-to-end approach designed specifically for businesses using PerfectCoaches.

PerfectCoaches is for Teams of Every Size

What would your organization be like if everybody did as well, and felt as well, as they could? What would society be like? An interesting feature of PerfectCoaches is that, despite the personal, perhaps intimate, aspects of self-awareness—even though the PerfectCoaches thought experiment is conducted in private—the method relies on interaction with others.

Because self-awareness arises from connecting with other people, personal connections and teams are key concepts in PerfectCoaches. Teams come in many sizes. No matter how large the group—two people, two hundred people, an entire organization, even a whole society—humans accomplish more by working as a team. To the extent that the people in any group have shared goals and clearly defined expectations of one another, they are not just individuals in a group—they are members of a team.

Two people interacting form a team if they share goals and expectations: mother and infant; best friends; intimate couples; co-workers or partners in business. Larger groups can also function well as a team, whether or not they interact face-to-face. The PerfectCoaches method enables a group to pursue the shared goals and clearly defined expectations that make them an effective team. Teams are important— not just at work but in every context, which is why building a winning life team is one of the best practices discussed in Chapter Seven.

You and other individuals who use the PerfectCoaches app put the key concepts into practice as a member of a team which may include a mentor, colleague, friend, or personal coach. An individual's skillset draws upon many sources, including:

- best practices identified by a company, university, or other organization
- skills taught in online or classroom training
- habits you observe in others
- best practices described in this book
- personal goals.

PerfectCoaches is especially powerful when used as an enterprise solution, meaning it can be used by organizations that want to increase workforce performance – or, in the case of a university, student performance - by providing everyone tools to achieve individual excellence and high-quality performance. Quality means that you and everyone on your team will not only have the skills to perform a task correctly, but also the habit of doing so consistently. Individual excellence contributes to improved performance throughout an organization, be it at a company, a university, or government agency.

PerfectCoaches is designed to foster quality at both the individual and enterprise levels. The *culture of quality* is also a *culture of coaching*, emphasizing guided development in everything from performance assessments to training programs. PerfectCoaches provides organizations with a consistent set of best practices that everyone, at every level, can use every day when working with customers and each other.

PerfectCoaches is for Enjoyment

PerfectCoaches is not only designed to become a habit, but also to be an *enjoyable* habit. It's a simple, powerful tool that can help you learn specific skills or change the entire trajectory of your life. It works best if you enjoy it and make it part of your daily routine. The first habit you master is the habit of making a brief journal entry every day that sums up your success for that day. You can, and should, have fun doing that, even on days when you didn't do as well as you might have hoped.

To emphasize that the PerfectCoaches method should be enjoyable, we have created a card game called *Got It! The PerfectCoaches Game*. The term "Got It!" refers to a feature in the app that lets you declare that you have mastered a new habit or skill.

Used either as a learning game or a party game, *Got It! The PerfectCoaches Game* is based on an advanced thought experiment, described in Chapter Nine, where you imagine famous leaders serving as coaches. In the game, "celebrity virtual coaches" players master best-practice habits, either as individuals or as members of a team. Interacting online with a virtual coach for the game is an optional feature.

Finally, although the book in your hand or on your screen may look like a workbook, it is designed to be a thoughtful, continuous "read" in the tradition of Dale Carnegie's *How to Win Friends and Influence People* or Stephen Covey's *The Seven Habits of Highly Effective People*. If you want to stop and delve into the specific habits discussed in the book, the app or the game may be a better place for you to do it.

You can use your phone or personal computer to access the PerfectCoaches app. Get started and see how the journal and virtual coach features work. Or just relax and settle in for an interesting read. Either way, enjoy!

Change One Thing Now

PerfectCoaches is an active process. It is something that you DO. For those who enjoy learning via short exercises, here is the first in a series inviting you to try the PerfectCoaches method as you read how it works. We will also provide a fictional person who faces these challenges as an example in the book.

Consider two important habits: being punctual and listening without interrupting. Are you often apologizing for running late? Do you interrupt others in professional or personal conversations?

Being self-aware will make you *mindful* of these *behaviors,* paving the way for mastering skills like punctuality and listening to others. Pay close attention to the PerfectCoaches thinking as you read and consider those habits you want to change.

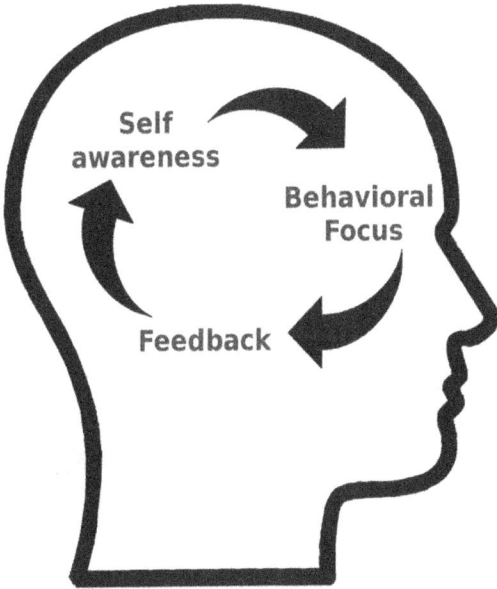

Part One

Self Awareness

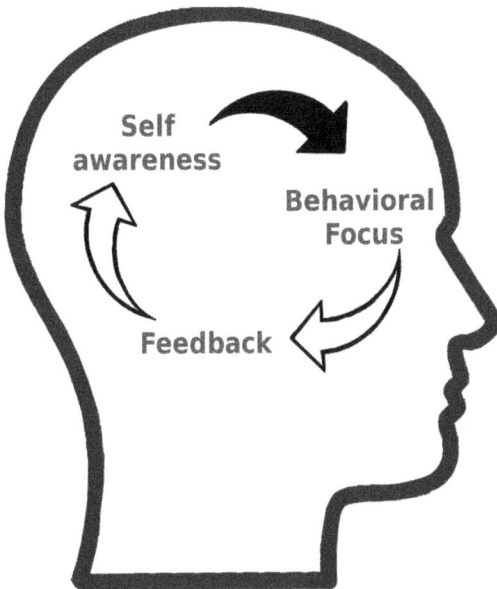

Chapter Two
This is Me

Imagine this scenario: Jane often runs late to everything, including her hard-won job as a junior attorney at a law firm. Her supervisor admonishes her and Jane vows to be on time (maybe even early) on Monday. She sets her alarm Sunday night, telling herself before she goes to sleep that this time, she won't hit the Snooze button, because that's what ends up making her late. The alarm goes off at six, Jane hits Snooze without thinking about it, and ends up being late. Again. When she gets to work, she is frustrated with herself for once again clocking in late and putting her job in jeopardy. Why does she undermine herself every day, especially when she knows how important being on time is for a job, she worked so hard to get? The answer escapes her.

Sound familiar? Most of us do things that we know are detrimental to our health, careers, goals, and relationships. What we don't know is why or, even more importantly, how to change those things. The key to living a life that supports and enriches your health, careers, goals, and relationships is *self-awareness*.

A human being can spend a lifetime inside his or her skin without truly knowing the person who is "wearing it". PerfectCoaches can help you clearly see the person you are, perhaps for the first time. This self-awareness, defined simply as knowing who you are, is valuable. In addition, PerfectCoaches builds upon self-awareness to help you be more mindful of your behavior. These are two important words.

> The key to living a life that supports and enriches your health, careers, goals, and relationships is *self-awareness*.

The first word, *mindful*, has various meanings in psychology as well as Buddhism, Hinduism, and other philosophical systems. PerfectCoaches uses a simple definition that is consistent with its use in most contexts:

Mindfulness is a clear, purposefulness awareness of the events taking place right now, in the present moment.

The second word, *behavior*, is defined in psychology as *the actions by which an organism adjusts to its environment*. PerfectCoaches uses behavior as an all-encompassing term for everything you do including skills, habits, activities, and inner experiences. Skills, which are behaviors learned and practiced in order to perform some specific task, are especially important in PerfectCoaches.

Behavior is defined in psychology as the actions by which an organism adjusts to its environment.

Our actions adjusts to, and in that sense are at least partially controlled by, the environment. PerfectCoaches emphasizes the importance of this fact. We adapt and change our behaviors based on where we are, who we are with, and what is expected of us. We often do this without thinking about it, which is where the lack of self-awareness comes into play.

PerfectCoaches uses the *Socratic method*. Socrates, one of history's great philosophers, had a method of continuously asking question after question without providing answers himself. The other person would discover contradictions in what he said and see what nonsensical conclusions were reached as Socrates pressed false assumptions to their logical conclusion. Socrates knew the questions he asked would eventually uncover the truth of the matter.

PerfectCoaches personifies fundamental inquiries about life as Coaches asking the questions. The questions themselves are based on "the question words" found in Rudyard Kipling's *The Elephant's Child*:

> *I Keep six honest serving-men*
> *(They taught me all I knew);*
> *Their names are What and Why and When*
> *And How and Where and Who.*

What, **When**, **Why**, **How**, **Where**, and **Who** are the fundamental fact-finding questions journalists, detectives, scientists, and others use to quickly understand the facts in a situation. PerfectCoaches adds a seventh question to the list: **What if**? This question encourages you to go beyond the facts to start exploring possibilities.

Here's how the PerfectCoaches thought experiment works—you ask yourself questions on a regular basis and, through those answers, gain self-awareness. With that self-awareness, you will be more mindful of your behavior and make choices that improve your life every single day.

Why Should I Ask Myself Questions?

A good coach doesn't tell his or her players what to do—he encourages them to think for themselves so that in the crush of a game, they have developed the instincts to pass or run. In short, to do whatever they need to do to win the game. PerfectCoaches doesn't come with a coach on the sidelines who is going to go over a playbook and watch post-game reels with you. That's because the only person you need on your team is already there—you.

Develop the habit of asking the questions, the 7 PerfectCoaches questions (see the box), and from those answers you gain insight, knowledge, and direction. You become, in a sense, your own coach. You're always there with yourself, so that built-in coaching is available all the time.

See how that works? The questions *are* the PerfectCoaches. The Coaches *are* the questions, and the questions *are* The Coaches. In the PerfectCoaches method, the term *The Coaches* is capitalized and treated as a proper noun because it's a one-of-a-kind thing, unique to you.

The Coaches you imagine as you are going through this book possess all the characteristics you

---

Life's 7 PerfectCoaches Questions

Keep these handy so you can refer to them often. These questions form the basis of the PerfectCoaches approach.

1. Who am I?
2. What do I do?
3. Why do I do it?
4. When do I do it best?
5. Where do I want to go?
6. How do I change?
7. What if I could change the world?

---

would seek in a person helping you develop as a professional and, just as importantly, as a person.

These questions *are* the Perfect Coaches. The Coaches *are* the questions, and the questions *are* The Coaches. In the PerfectCoaches method, the term *The Coaches* is capitalized and treated as a proper noun, a "one-of-a-kind thing".

They are not just any coaches. They are *perfect* coaches. In the dictionary sense, they are *entirely without flaws, defects, or shortcomings.* The Coaches you imagine possess all the characteristics you would seek in a person helping you develop as a professional and, just as important, as a person. The Coaches are:

- Perfectly patient.
- Perfectly focused on the future.
- Perfectly committed to simplicity.
- Perfectly disciplined.
- Perfectly at ease with the human condition.

Because PerfectCoaches is a thought experiment limited only by your imagination, you can take advantage of each of these characteristics.

Perfectly Patient

Patience is perhaps the most important quality for a sport or life coach. It is particularly important in the PerfectCoaches thought experiment, which can endure for a lifetime. Patience is the willingness to live with delay, a willingness to wait. Effective coaches are in it for the long haul.

> *Plants do not grow merely to satisfy ambitions or to fulfill good intentions. They thrive because someone expended effort on them.*
> — Liberty Hyde Bailey

With PerfectCoaches, you can thrive because of the effort that you and others expend on you.

Perfectly Focused on the Future

The Coaches begin the journey with you looking forward, not backward. One of the most consistent and enduring themes in literature dealing with personal development or, for that matter, organizational development is that each day can be a new start. Each day can be a time for improvement or even reinvention. The Coaches agree with the old saying, "Today is the first day of the rest of your life."

This focus on the future means The Coaches will never judge you based on what you did last year or yesterday. There are rules and laws to obey in life and failing to do so can have negative consequences. The Coaches can't change that, but they can help you keep setbacks or even disasters in perspective.

If you are a person who wants to be judged or believes that you should be judged, you can give one or even all your Coaches that responsibility. Sometimes being judged can bring a constructive sense of closure, as if to say, "All right, I did that. I admit it and now I can move on." Otherwise, in this method you will never be judged.

Perfectly Committed to Simplicity

The third source of their perfection is that The Coaches are committed to keeping things simple. Less is more. They embrace a principle known as Occam's razor, which favors describing or explaining a phenomenon by using the fewest possible concepts. Here, important concepts like mindfulness are used in their simplest form. Their meaning is mostly self-evident and can be explored through concrete examples.

This emphasis on simplicity is at the heart of PerfectCoaches. For example, the PerfectCoaches app is built to be simple and straightforward. Whether you access it via a personal computer or mobile device, you build self-awareness quickly with a few short questions. Your journal entries should be short and simple. The questions you receive as feedback are short and thought-provoking—a trimmed-down version of a Socratic dialog.

Perfectly Disciplined

The Coaches are also perfectly disciplined. In this method, discipline refers to staying on track to achieve a well-defined goal. Discipline involves knowing what needs to be done and doing it. It doesn't mean that The Coaches are "disciplinarians" in a negative sense—

stern, unyielding or just plain mean, which the term discipline might imply to some people. Rather, it means that they are focused on goals and progress, serving as models for the self-discipline that you can achieve. True discipline in life is self-discipline.

Perfectly at Ease with the Human Condition

Finally, The Coaches are perfectly at ease with the human condition and, for that matter, the world as it is. They completely accept the idea that life is a struggle and that every human being lives imperfectly in an imperfect world. Just as The Coaches do not judge or condemn *you*, they do not judge or condemn the world.

Ironically, understanding that the world is imperfect and accepting the world as it is makes it easier to envision what would happen if you *could* change it. In other words, instead of pretending the world is without its many problems, or simply wishing it were, face the world as it presents itself in this moment and do what you can to make yourself better and, if possible, make the world around you a better place.

PerfectCoaches enables a process for making small sustainable changes to the world just as you can make small, sustainable changes to yourself. In fact, most modern enterprises where the skills of leaders, salespeople, and customer service staff are valued, suggestions for change are encouraged. The PerfectCoaches journal enables not just individual excellence but enterprise performance and quality, simply by asking the question: "What if…?"

PerfectCoaches is a *virtuous cycle*, a series of events which reinforce themselves through what is sometimes called a *self-amplifying feedback loop*. In a virtuous cycle, things keep getting better because each step not only brings improvement but sets the stage for further improvement. The cycle can bring benefits in individuals, teams, and organizations where they practice their profession.

Everyone will interact with this book and the app according to their own preferences. Yet the process is always the same. It begins with asking questions that create self-awareness. Self-awareness, in turn, makes it easier for you to focus on specific behaviors you want to change. Finally, feedback and reinforcement create the path for continuous growth.

No matter if you are writing in the Pen and Paper Workbook or using the app as you read this book, blurt out the first things that come to mind. Psychologists call this free association. By answering off the top of your head, you are less likely to consider how other people might react to your answers and more likely to say what you really think or feel.

This first pass through the questions is a snapshot. You are not sitting for a portrait. Rather, you are snapping a selfie that is meant to be candid and revealing. The answers can be as short as a tweet. If you refine your answers later, they will become more precise and meaningful, but they can remain short.

As you get started, particularly if you are using the PerfectCoaches app, don't be self-conscious or allow the process to feel like hard work. You aren't sitting down in a classroom somewhere to take a test that has right and wrong answers. You are not completing some sort of personality profile for a new job. Rather, you are taking time to learn about yourself.

Picture yourself in a pleasant place—say, a quiet park on a sunny afternoon—talking to The Coaches. Each, in their turn, will ask you to think about an important question. You'll quickly jot down the first few answers that come to mind. Getting started at all is what counts. You'll be able to come back as often as you like to add more.

PerfectCoaches is based on self-awareness, behavioral focus, and feedback. You can perfect the process every day by focusing on at least one thing you want to start, stop, or improve. Self-awareness sets the stage for mindfulness and behavioral focus, and feedback sustains the focus. The process works because you make it work. Perfect, i.e., perfecting the process, *is* possible.

Who Am I?

"Know Thyself." – Socrates

This is perhaps life's single most important question. Knowing the answer helps make sense out of what otherwise would be a jumble of disjointed experiences and feelings. Many people pose the question to themselves but can't quite figure out how to find the answer. PerfectCoaches can help.

Who are you, right now, right this minute?

Don't overthink your answer, just write down the first thoughts that come to mind, either in the workbook or in the app, or on a pad of paper. Your answer to this first question is your understanding of who you are, written spontaneously in the first words that come to you.

People find the self-awareness snapshot challenging if they overthink their answers. In the initial pass through the questions, it's more productive and enjoyable to give quick, off-the-cuff answers. This first question is designed to put you in touch with your *core self.*

Your core self is the animating force in your day-to-day life, revealed in who you are and what you do.

To understand the source of your energy is a valuable insight in its own right. No matter how you answer this question, you are describing the face you glimpse in a mirror, sometimes vaguely, sometimes with great clarity. When you look in the mirror, you will see a person who can be defined in three ways: the roles you play, specific behaviors that you and others see, and private inner experiences. People often answer the question "Who Am I?" in the following order, reflecting the way PerfectCoaches defines the ways we view the self.

Roles

In regular life, people introduce themselves to others by naming socially defined categories that could be a checkbox on a questionnaire. After saying their name, a person might say, "I am a manager," "I am an American," and "I am a student," are examples. Playing a "role" like manager or student ultimately involves specific behaviors, and roles are labels, that group behaviors together. Simply naming the roles you play is a quick, convenient way to see the big picture of your place in life.

Behaviors

You are what you repeatedly do. To say that your self consists of *behaviors* is to say that, in one sense, you are the specific skills, activities, and habits that people who know you well, or observe you in action, could list. "I talk fast," "I go back to my hometown for holidays," "I always refer to Wikipedia," and "I eat lunch at my desk" are examples.

Inner Experiences

And finally, your self consists of *inner experiences* that are private to you. "I enjoy working in teams," "I'm afraid of failing math," "I'm angry all the time because people don't know what they are doing," and "I dread seeing the quarterly results," are examples.

Inner experiences can be thought of as behaviors. They are things you do. What makes them different is that they are things you do that others can't see. They are things you are feeling and thoughts you are having inside, and they can sometimes manifest themselves in behavior seen by others, like the expressions on your face.

Attempting to express those experiences in words sets the stage for improving "mind sight", the ability to understand the thoughts and feelings that drive behavior in both your professional and personal life.

What Do I Do?

> *"We are what we repeatedly do. Excellence, therefore, is not an act but a habit." – Aristotle*

Your answer to the question, "Who am I?" describes the big picture of your core self. In PerfectCoaches, it is basically an essay that you write about how you see yourself at a given moment.

Your core self is also revealed in the small details of what you actually do. PerfectCoaches is about understanding your behaviors, activities, habits, and skills. Your capacity to develop each day by changing one behavior at a time is enhanced when you see each behavior in the context of your total self.

The actions you take and the roles you fulfill are the ingredients of your life. The answer to this question is factual. If you had a camera and microphone follow you around the clock, wherever you went, it would record what you do. PerfectCoaches wants you to become aware of what you are doing, as if you were commenting on the 24x7 video. After watching yourself 24x7 for, let's say a month, could you develop a list of the top ten things you do, either because they are important or because you do them often?

Who you are and what you do are, in many respects, flip sides of the same coin. You can describe what you do in terms of roles you play, specific behaviors that you and others can see, and *inner experiences*.

Although the app only asks you to name the five most important things you do, if you tried to list everything you do, the list would seem endless. Here is a list of possible answers to the question:

Roles

- Parent
- Sibling
- Manager
- Salesperson
- Leader
- Co-worker
- Student

Behaviors

- Study
- Conduct meetings
- Remember names and faces
- Greet people with a smile
- Attend meetings
- Spend time with family
- Work out
- Read

Inner Experiences

- Be happy
- Be sad
- Be angry
- Be amused
- Be afraid

Whether you are using the app, online tool, or a piece of paper, three or four answers like these are fine as an initial snapshot.

Why Do I Do It?

> *"Begin everything with the end in mind."* – Stephen Covey

This is where you begin to analyze and take the first steps toward change. Imagine someone interviewing you and asking simply, "Why do you do what you do?" Or imagine an *inner accountant* constantly asking, "Why are you doing that? Have you really considered the costs and rewards associated with each thing you do?"

For each of the things you do, try to identify the predominate reason you have for doing it. You may do a thing for more than one reason, but it is important that you at least understand the predominant reason, such as:

- For money
- For fame
- For fun
- To prove that you can
- To help you grow professionally
- To please your friends
- To feel like a woman or a man
- To serve your company
- To feel responsible
- To prove mindfulness counts
- To meet basic needs

Asking why you do things can help you identify actions and behaviors that are done for no reason or the wrong reason. As will be discussed later, this same concept in Business Process Reengineering (BPR) is used to eliminate what are called "non-value-added" activities.

Psychologists offer theories of motivation to explain why people do things. One of the most enduring ideas is Abraham Maslow's *hierarchy of needs.* According to Maslow, the first needs you are motivated to meet involve survival, i.e., physiological requirements for food, water, and comfort and the need for safety and security. Next come social needs for intimacy, friendship, prestige, and a sense of accomplishment. Once physiological and social needs are met, the need to fulfill one's highest potential, the need for *self-actualization,* becomes your primary motivator.

Your inner accountant might want to draw upon this idea and ask if basic needs, social needs, or the more complex need for self-actualization explain why you do each thing you do.

When Do I Do It Best?

> *"Always do your best. What you plant now*
> *you will harvest later." – Og Mandino*

Each of us can develop an *inner craftsman,* always asking if this is the best work you can do. To excel at the things you do, it pays to know when you do them best. The question doesn't refer to the time of day, but rather the conditions under which you do a thing best. There are a lot of ways to identify when you do something best. Here are a few:

- When I am eager to do it
- When I want to get it over with
- In the morning
- In the evening
- Before eating
- After eating
- With other people
- By myself
- Right at the deadline
- When I have practiced

The concept of doing something "best" implies that your behavior has been evaluated. In social psychology, the concept of the *looking-glass self* says that we *see ourselves* through the mirror of how we think *others see us.*

When we evaluate how well we do, we are to some extent using other people's standards. This begins when parents and caretakers correct us or praise us as children. In professional life, you are in fact being evaluated by others. As will be discussed later, this feedback is important.

PerfectCoaches invites you to be mindful of the standards used by others, but to also set your own standards. These may be the same standards other people apply, but they do not have to be. You decide on the standards, and it is up to you to apply them.

Change One Thing Now

Jane, the always tardy lawyer, wants to change but doesn't know how. This simple exercise can make all the difference for her (and anyone else who wants to change one behavior right now). Ask yourself:

"*Why* do I want to be punctual?"

(Change that to tidy, or organized, or whatever you want to change).

Then list the moments **when** you do this best. Are there circumstances and behavioral cues that help you arrive on time and finish assignments on time? How can you use this information to better meet every deadline and appointment?

Chapter Three
This is Possible

At this point PerfectCoaches shifts emphasis from the present "As-Is" you (what you now do, why you do it, and when you do it best) to the future "To-Be" you (where you are going, and how you change in order to get there).

Where Am I Going?

> *"It is not in the stars to hold our destiny but in ourselves."* - William Shakespeare

As Oprah Winfrey said, "Right now you are one choice away from a new beginning." There is a question, however: The beginning of *what*? Many people never have a "vision of a future self" that is vivid enough to help them plan for their life or their career. Think of your career as a journey toward a destination. Your career is a central part of your life, and it may be true that your career is driving your life and your future.

Throughout life, parents, teachers, coaches, friends, intimates, and others make plans for us. Ultimately, of course, it is your responsibility to plan your life and act upon that plan. Imagine that you have an *inner planner* who keeps saying, "Hey, you need a game plan for life."

There is an old adage, "If you don't know where you're going, any bus will take you there." You should have at least a general concept of where you want to go in life, and who you want to become. In some cases, it is perhaps even more important to know where you do not want to go and who you do not want to be or become.

Perhaps you are truly troubled by a lot of bad habits and do not want to stay that way. Perhaps your career is in a rut, and you want to get out. When you say where you want to go in life, feel free to say also where you do *not* want to go. Especially when you are young, it is important to avoid choices that will set you on a path you do not want to follow.

How Do I Change?

> *"I hear and I forget. I see and I remember.*
> *I do and I understand."* – Confucius

Perhaps there is indeed a core self that stays nearly constant throughout life, yet the fact is we are always changing, sometimes for the better, sometimes for the worse. Although building self-awareness and mindfulness are important goals, the fulcrum of PerfectCoaches is a reliable method for purposefully changing what you do. How do you change your career in order to become the "To-Be Me" envisioned by an inner planner? Or, for that matter, how can you change something you named when you answered the question, "What do I do?"

The coach who helps you focus on making changes in your career and your behavior is the *virtual coach*. In the PerfectCoaches thought experiment, you can imagine this to be a real or fictional person chosen by you to play the role. Or you can use your online journal to maintain a dialog with the virtual coach feature that comes with a subscription to PerfectCoaches.

The virtual coach will facilitate your effort to improve the quality of your professional life by engaging you in a dialog about specific behaviors to add, eliminate, or improve. If you truly believe that you are what you repeatedly do, then changing yourself ultimately comes down to changing what you do.

When posing the question, "How Do I Change?" the first clarifying question in the dialogue is "change what?"

People often try to change a lot of things at once, a complete "makeover". PerfectCoaches focuses on changing one "target" behavior at a time.

Changing behavior involves stopping something you are doing because doing it is not consistent with the person you want to be, starting something new because it is what you want to do, or doing something you already do, only better. Discussed below are several simple ways to begin the process of changing behavior. They are not mutually exclusive. If you want to change your behavior, you can do one or more of the following:

Imitate

Use another person or the best practices discussed throughout this book as a model. Studies have shown that children will imitate adults or other children performing a specific activity. Adults choose role models for themselves, and in some sense, imitate what their role models do. Imitation is the sincerest form of flattery.

Substitute

One simple way to change is to substitute one behavior for another. For example, if you want to drink less soda or alcohol, drink a glass of water instead. If you want to keep doing something but do it better, you can substitute one way of doing it for another. Here your inner craftsman's question concerning when you do it best offers useful ideas.

Change Scripts

The "scripts" for roles we play determine what we do. They are the words we speak and actions we take that fit the role we see ourselves in. According to this "dramaturgic model", people perform one or more roles each day as if they were on a stage.

You can learn an entirely new role by adopting behaviors that you believe are consistent with it. For example, if you are promoted to manager, you may begin to behave differently toward members of your team because you are now their manager, not their peer. Or, if you are already a manager and want to become more effective, you may adopt new behaviors you believe are those of an effective manager.

Train

Training and formal lessons usually teach specific behaviors required to perform a specific task. Formal training, either in person or virtually (as in an online course), can be an effective way to change behaviors and learn new ones, especially when the behaviors are clearly identified and used after the training is complete.

PerfectCoaches is an extremely useful supplement to formal training because you can practice new behaviors after the training is complete. This works best if you can define the behavior as a thing, you either do or do not perform. This lets you measure your success.

Increase Perspective and Mindfulness

Your inner accountant's question, "Why do I do it?" can help you gain perspective on the inner experiences that motivate things you do.

There are theories and approaches that say you can change behavior by gaining perspective on your emotions and inner thoughts. Early practitioners of this view include Sigmund Freud, Karl Jung, Viktor Frankl, and Carl Rogers.

Many thinkers and writers today emphasize the importance of mindfulness. Being mindful allows you to understand why you behave in certain ways and the impact your actions have on people and situations.

New behaviors stay and old behaviors go because of their consequences. Once you've decided on the behavior to change and your strategy for changing it, you can begin to focus on the conditions under which the behavior is most likely to change. This is where the psychological concept of reinforcement and the related concept of antecedents, or triggers, enter the picture.

As you focus on changing a behavior, pay attention first to the events, or triggers, that seem to bring it out, and second, what happens next—i.e., the consequences of the behavior that reinforce it.

Understand Reinforcement and Cues

Reinforcement means that rewarding a behavior makes it more likely, while punishing or ignoring it makes it less likely. What happens after you do something will influence whether you do it again. No matter how you choose your target behavior or skill, the next challenge is to make it a habit. This requires you to be aware of the triggers (cues, antecedents, and discriminative stimuli) and the reinforcements (rewards and punishments) that influence what you do.

Cues are things that happen in your environment before or while you do something. To improve your chances of making change stick, eliminate or avoid cues for the behavior you want to stop. In other words, make it as easy as possible for you to perform the desirable behavior while making it difficult to perform the undesirable behavior.

Change One Thing Now

Jane, the always tardy lawyer, can use these techniques to help improve her punctuality. She already knows the consequences for being late—not getting a promotion and possibly being fired.

She imitates another lawyer in the office by mimicking his timeliness. He often arrives early at meetings, and she shifts her behavior to do the same. She substitutes being early for being late, and realizes what cues cause her to be tardy, such as putting on the television while getting ready (which distracts her and makes her late). When she struggles to be on time, she reminds herself of her upcoming performance review, and the good performance bonus she is working to receive.

Now it's your turn. Ask yourself: **What behavior do I want to change?**

Now, make a list of people whose behavior you can imitate, what substitutions you can make, the reinforcements and cues that help or hinder you, and the consequences of your behaviors.

Understand the Consequences of Behavior

Similar approaches apply for the consequences of behavior. Here, you provide only positive reinforcement/rewards for the new behavior *and* provide either no reinforcement, or negative reinforcement for the undesirable behavior.

Managing the conditions under which behavior takes place is something you perfect as you use PerfectCoaches. Feedback received via your journal moves the process forward until you make the journal entry that says, "GOT IT!" and the new habit becomes part of your skillset.

What if I Could Change the World?

*"Perfection is not attainable, but if we chase perfection
we can catch excellence." – Vince Lombardi*

The world shapes us. From earliest childhood, we learn habits based on the consequences of what we do. The question "How do I change?" takes on additional meaning when you are mindful of the fact that what you do, and what you are *able* and *permitted* to do, is constrained by the world in which you live and work. Could you change that world, thereby opening new opportunities to excel and get things done?

This question is important for three reasons. First, when you closely examine your thoughts on how you would change the world, you learn about yourself. Your vision of a perfect world is, in many respects, a projection of your vision of a perfect self, and you should study both visions side by side.

Second, defining and pursuing possibilities is a hallmark of leadership. Leaders often ask, *"What if we defined and solved this problem in this particular way."* Leaders also encourage the same kind of thinking from those they hope to lead and inspire.

The third reason this question is important is that you *can* change the world. Think of what you would want the world to be if you could change it. It can be a sweeping change that affects all of humanity, or it could be a change in the way your company or school does business. Often, it is better to begin by asking *what if* you could make simple changes to how people interact or how things get done. Any journal entry you make while you are considering how the world could be better can begin with one simple question:

"What if…?"

The same principles of self-awareness and behavioral focus that apply when you change what you do are also useful when you are trying to change a situation or process that involves other people or a larger enterprise. You can ask questions like "What if we eliminated upper management approval for purchases under $100?" or "What if we could take practice tests online and get the results right away?"

As you become more self-aware, you will become mindful of the environment around you. That mindfulness enables you to see that there are some things that would make the world better—not just for you, but for others as well. Some things you might want to change are outside of the scope of what your immediate team, organization, or community can do.

Even when they are small changes in, say, the procedures used by your work team, these are often things you cannot accomplish alone. When that is the case, simply ask the question "What if?" at the beginning of a journal entry.

This will alert you and the virtual coach to the fact that there is an opportunity for improvement outside of your boundaries. It will also motivate you to get that process started. In some instances, you may be able to lead that process, using the best practices for leadership discussed in the book.

The PerfectCoaches app can be used as a "24x7 virtual suggestion box" or, better yet, a "24x7 virtual Kaizen." Kaizen is a Japanese word for the practice of continuous improvement in business. It means "good change", and usually involves specific changes suggested by individuals or teams at Kaizen events, typically workshops where problems are identified, and corrective actions proposed.

Big results can come from small changes that get their start from a journal entry that simply begins "What if…?"

Part Two

Behavioral Focus

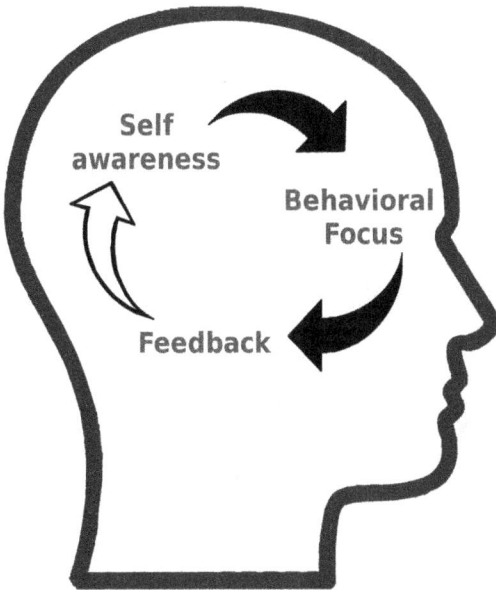

Chapter Four
Personal Excellence

Using PerfectCoaches can change the whole path, the whole trajectory, of your life, but it does not require big changes or huge commitments. You simply must be aware that there are always opportunities to change yourself and then focus on the behaviors, the habits, that will make that happen.

Even if your organization has adopted PerfectCoaches as an enterprise performance tool, the process itself belongs to you. You decide how to use it, how to perfect it, and what changes you want to make.

Getting that first snapshot of who you are is a useful and enjoyable experience in its own right. Plus, it sets the stage for becoming the person you want to be, one habit at a time. Habit, after all, is the flywheel of society, as suggested in the quote from William James at the beginning of this book. As you build self-awareness and change what you do, you perfect the virtuous cycle.

PerfectCoaches is about doing. The philosopher Confucius said, *I hear and I forget. I see and I remember. I do and I understand.* The simple act of starting your PerfectCoaches snapshot—either in the Pen and Paper Workbook or using the app, or both—moves you toward the understanding that only comes from *doing.* By writing thoughtful answers, you are actively interacting with the questions.

Not only is PerfectCoaches about *doing,* but it is also about being *mindful* of what you are doing. As noted earlier, the word "mindful" is used in psychology and practices associated with Zen and other philosophical traditions. It takes on different shades of meaning depending on the context in which it is used, but it always involves:

- Being attentive to the present;
- Being objective and maintaining an emotional distance from events; and
- Being aware of all the many factors, including people, involved in an issue.

Our definition of mindfulness—a *clear, purposeful awareness of the events taking place right now, in the present moment*—is compatible with most uses of the term. Mindfulness, self-awareness, and behavioral focus all work together in PerfectCoaches. Because being mindful is crucial for the successful use of PerfectCoaches, going through this process in turn helps you learn the habit of being mindful.

There are many roles to be played and jobs to be performed in our homes, schools, workplaces, social occasions, etc. It is possible to be mindful of what we do by staying focused on each task and doing it in the best way we can, i.e., by following *best practices.*

Like the ideas of the "As-Is" self and "To-Be" self, the concept of best practices is adapted from the discipline of BPR. Reengineering asks, "If we were starting over today, how would we design our company?" and "What other company does this particular task best?" That is the source of best practices. You can think of a best-practice as a successful behavior you saw other people perform and decided to imitate, as we talked about in the last chapter.

Within BPR, PerfectCoaches would be called "a repeatable solution", meaning that the process is well-defined, well-understood, and effective. You, however, are not a business. You are a person. Nevertheless, many BPR concepts are useful. For example, asking *why* you do something enables you to eliminate activities that aren't helpful and may even be harmful. Taking that step would be similar to what BPR practitioners call eliminating non-value-added activities.

The idea of "best practices" can be adapted, with suitable modifications, to individual careers. Ask simply:

"If I was going to start over today, what habits, skills, and activities would I emphasize?"

That will help you make decisions and changes in the future.

Additionally, by asking *when* you do something best, you can make useful behaviors even more effective. This also is like process improvement in BPR.

Best practices promote *quality,* which is another concept frequently used in BPR projects. We have a specific definition of quality in a business setting:

Quality can be defined as the absence of defects or significant variability.

All the best practices discussed in *PerfectCoaches* ultimately produce quality outcomes. For work and learning, it means consistently achieving intellectual satisfaction and rigor. Best practices in nutrition, fitness, and health foster quality of life and a consistent, focused sense of high-level wellness.

PerfectCoaches helps you master one best-practice behavior at a time. You continuously practice each one you master as you move onto the next skill you want to master. One skill builds on another. For that reason, PerfectCoaches calls a set of best practices a skillset.

PerfectCoaches enables you to "neatly arrange" the best practices, one behavior at a time, to create the person you want to become. The app displays all the skills, behaviors, and habits you have mastered and continue to use each time it is appropriate to do so that you can see the stack grow as you go along.

You can also think of your *Skillset Résumé.* The word *résumé* comes from the French, meaning "summarize". As a business concept, your Skillset Résumé summarizes your core skills and is another way to communicate who you are and what you do. Although your journal displays the stack of behaviors, you acquired as a simple "Got It" list, the graphic below portrays a stack of mastered skills as if it were a *résumé* that you would print and show others.

Doing this gives you a way to implement your own standards of quality performance by doing each task correctly (reducing defects) and doing it the same way every time (reducing variation).

PerfectCoaches enables each person to build their own résumé of skills and habits. Here is mine:

1. I do my to-do list
2. I am on time for meetings, assignments, and getting back to people
3. I remember names after the initial introduction to people
4. I dress for success
5. I listen without interrupting
6. I engage my brain, paying attention and concentrating on the task at hand
7. I lead mindfully
8. I follow the rule "always be charming"
9. I follow the rule "always be confident"
10. I live life mindfully and holistically

We begin with five best-practice habits that can lay the foundation for a lifetime of successful time management, teamwork, and learning. Let's illustrate how mastering best practices is often easier if you strive for complete, 100% success. For each of the "first five" best practices, the question is posed: Did you do it every time? Yes or No.

You can conceptualize most best practices as something that you do every time or not, so you can modify the others presented in the book in a similar way. To learn the PerfectCoaches process, we encourage you to adopt all the following habits and behaviors that feel right for you.

Engage Your Brain: Thank It By Using It

> *"The chief function of the body is to carry
> the brain around." – Thomas Edison*

Learn to concentrate, to pay attention, to always *engage your brain* in the task at hand. This habit is one of the keys to success.

Your brain is the seat of self-awareness. It remembers things, creates new ideas, and processes the incoming data connecting you to your teams and the world. It's there to be used.

Engage your brain by giving each thing you do your full attention. That's the best way to demonstrate that you appreciate its power. Not only is your brain quite possibly your best friend and greatest asset, but it is also an asset for your team. Give yourself a little tap to the forehead to be sure to use it at every meeting, every chance you get. Especially when you head into large meetings or classes where you are mostly a passive listener, it may be helpful to simply remind yourself to "bring your brain". Or, for fun, look around and ask yourself if the other people brought *their* brain to the meeting.

When you compare your brain to a computer, don't think about your laptop or desktop. Instead, think about the greatest supercomputer ever built. As a human, you are endowed with an incredibly efficient information processor. Weighing just three pounds (about 2% of your body weight), it shares approximately 2,000 calories in energy per day with all your other muscles and organs. It's incredibly efficient; your whole body is using the energy it would take to power a single light bulb, whereas supercomputers use energy that would power whole city blocks. And unlike conventional computers, your brain has an infinite number of connections and can generate new ones on its own because, unlike a computer, your brain—and you—are alive.

Don't just engage your brain, thank it. Wait, *thank* your brain? Why not? There it is, working away between your ears and behind your eyes. Not only does it remember things, not only does it create ideas, but it also processes the enormous volume of incoming data— sights, sounds, smells, tastes, scents, sensations of touch, and bodily motion—that you use to move through the world each day.

Heightening the powers of this information processing wonder are the connections it makes. There's your spinal cord, a powerful system, even though it is only about the diameter of your middle finger. Tracts of nerves within your spinal cord carry input from the sensory organs to your brain. Tracts of nerves exiting your brain control the whole show, carrying the output information that initiates muscle movement and controls bodily functions.

Also exiting your brain are your cranial nerves which (at some risk of oversimplification) manage how your face, mouth, nose, and head perform. The facial expressions that give clues to your *inner experiences* are controlled by these cranial nerves.

Just as you tap your forehead as a reminder to engage your brain, thanking your brain with a small gesture like a pat on the forehead can also be a good idea. You can also thank your brain by exercising it. Exercising your muscles improves their capabilities, and exercising your brain improves its capabilities and the quality of what it produces.

The concept of quality thinking in a business sense takes on additional meaning in the 21st century because there is a growing awareness that our human brains are competing with computer brains in the labor force itself. The July/August 2015 edition of *Foreign Affairs,* for example, has a cover picture of a robot with the caption "Hi Robot". Gideon Rose introduces the issue by noting that as the fields of automation and artificial intelligence evolve, fears have mounted over the potential for robots to "threaten our jobs, our purpose, and our very self- definition as human."

The human brain is a powerful thing, so each of us should learn how to use it to its fullest potential, if for no other reason than because computer-based intelligent systems like IBM's Watson can already do certain things (e.g., play chess) better than the top human champion.

Plus, the idea of improvement lies at the foundation of PerfectCoaches. As a child, your brain began to acquire the capacity to do things like remember people's names. Yet this is a skill

> We often regret being late, but rarely do we regret being early.

that can be sharpened through adolescence and into adulthood. PerfectCoaches is designed to help you do new things and improve the things you already do. Don't be afraid to exercise your brain as if it were a muscle, that responds well to a vigorous workout.

For a large part of our lives, especially when we're young, that brain we treasure is more than a nice thing to have. Rather, it's a major resource, perhaps a weapon even, in a battle to learn what the world believes you should know. That battle is called studying, and you win it with learning as your signature skill.

When you study, your brain is acquiring a relatively well-defined set of facts and concepts. Often, though not always, that set is defined by someone else. Here, it's like your brain is marching down a path, sometimes well marked, sometimes dimly lit, and sometimes having the feel of an obstacle course designed for maximum frustration.

Occasionally, you study facts and concepts of your own choosing. In this case, you have given yourself an assignment. Deadlines and other criteria for success are self-imposed. Now your brain can hum tra-la-la and skip down the path, pausing at your own discretion to concentrate on a fact or concept that is particularly interesting. No matter what you are learning or why you are learning it, you are exercising your brain.

Did you give your forehead a little tap to engage it when appropriate, and to thank it, perhaps at the end of the day, to acknowledge all your brain did for you today? Yes, or No?

Do Your To-Do List

> *"The human animal differs from the lesser primates in his passion for lists." – H. Allen Smith*

Not only should you engage your brain in everything you do, you should also make sure you get everything done that needs to get done. We call this doing your to-do list.

Successful professionals are effective managers of that very precious resource—their own time.

For students, studying effectively requires that time be used wisely. The time-honored to-do list is an essential tool for seasoned professionals, students, or anyone who understands the importance of time management. Having a written to-do list is important (see Appendix 2 for examples), but it's more important to *do* what is on it.

A 2011 article by Masicampo and Baumeister in *The Journal of Personality and Social Psychology* cited research that college students pursue an average of fifteen goals at any one time. In a series of experiments that demonstrated the benefit of having a specific plan of action and completing tasks, Masicampo and Baumeister concluded that getting tasks off the agenda "can free cognitive resources for other tasks", improving overall performance.

> Use a to-do list to unclutter your mind.

There is a lively debate about the value of to-do lists, but most writers seem to agree that an effective to-do list doesn't clutter your mind with too many things to do, but rather *clears* it by letting you get things done and off your mind. In other words, their real value emerges when you complete tasks on the list. That is why short lists of three to five items that can be completed are the most useful.

Did you do your to-do list today? Yes, or No?

Be Punctual

> *"I could never have done what I have done without the habits of punctuality, order, and diligence."*
> – Thomas Edison

Getting things done is important. It is also important to do them on time. Effective time managers know the value of being punctual.

Arriving on time for classes, meetings, and social occasions is good manners. You are being courteous to others. You are also being courteous *to yourself* because punctuality is a habit which, like a to-do list, can unclutter your mind as you go through the day.

There are different ways to achieve this goal. One approach is simply planning to arrive ten minutes early. If traveling is involved, think of best-case, worst-case, and likely scenarios for traveling time. Then go with the likely case, not the best case, as many people do. If the meeting or social occasion is crucial, plan for the worst-case travel time.

**Punctual means happening or doing
something at the agreed or proper time.**

Punctuality is not limited to arriving for events on time. Being punctual also means submitting documents or assignments on the prescribed schedule. In addition, it applies to "getting back to people" at a specific time. Many organizations have formal standards for returning calls or answering questions for customers within one or two days. It is a good practice to set such standards for yourself in replying to phone or text messages from friends, family, and colleagues.

Completing assignments on schedule and arriving on time every time is not just polite; it can help you succeed. Punctuality is a habit, which, like a to-do list, unclutters your thoughts so you can "engage your brain" and pay attention to what you are doing right now.

Did you do everything on time today? Yes, or No?

Listen Without Interrupting

*"There is no greater rudeness than to interrupt another
in the current of his discourse." – John Locke*

We have two ears and one mouth, all with their own pathway to the brain, and it can be argued that the ears-to-brain circuit is the most important one for effective communication. An amazing variety of books on all sorts of subjects from sales to leadership to success in marriage emphasize the importance of listening. For example, Craig

Lawn's *Shut up and Sell: How to Say Less and Sell More* is a classic in the world of sales where such things as the best talk/listen ratio of 2 to 1 (i.e., the potential buyer should talk twice the amount of the salesperson) is hotly debated.

The verb "listen" is used a lot, but its true definition, *to pay attention, heed,* is often overlooked. Be mindful of the need to heed, and be prepared to act upon what the other person is saying. Become a better leader, colleague, and, yes, friend or intimate, by simply looking at the speaker and listening attentively without judging or interrupting. Train yourself to never, or at least rarely, interrupt.

> Engaging your brain and getting things done on time are the gateway skills for individual achievement. *Listening* is the gateway skill for getting things done with other people.

Did you go through your day listening attentively without interrupting others? Yes, or No?

Do Everything for a Purpose

"Rise each day with this steadfast goal: Do only those things you know are worth doing." – Anonymous

PerfectCoaches invites you to ask yourself why you do the things you do. It can be fun, but also instructive, to try the thought experiment of conversing with an inner accountant who asks pointed questions about what might seem to be wastes of your time, energy, and money. For example, that inner accountant might see you monitoring the news on your phone constantly and ask, "What is the purpose of that?"

For each thing you did today, did you ask if the rewards it brought for you and others were worth the time and energy invested? Yes, or No?

> You have 24 hours in a day. Don't waste a minute doing things that aren't worth doing.

Each profession requires its own combination of knowledge, skills, and abilities. The skills discussed under the heading of professional excellence vary from one profession to the next, from one organization to the next.

Similarly, the challenges of professional life, beginning in school and university, vary from one person to the next. For each person, they vary from one time to the next. Each person meets each challenge in their own way. These skills are broadly applicable across organizations, professions, and phase of life.

Remember Names

"Forgive your enemies, but never forget their names."
– John F. Kennedy

Mary Kay Ash, the founder of Mary Kay cosmetics, wrote, "Everyone has an invisible sign hanging from their neck saying, 'Make me feel important.' Never forget this message when working with people." In the same vein, she also said, "No matter how busy you are, you must take time to make the other person feel important." She considered caring and kindness to be the essential ingredients of a successful workforce. Her book, *The Mary Kay Way*, first published in 1984, is still a useful source for best-practice behaviors.

When introduced to people, pretend they handed you a business card. Remember their name; don't throw the card away. There are systems for improving your memory, but the first step is to be mindful of the fact that calling people by name makes them feel valued.

Did you remember the names of the people you met today? Yes, or No?

Understand the Other Person's Point of View

"You never really understand a person until you consider things from his point of view." – Harper Lee

Effective sales, service, and leadership, even friendship, require seeing the other person's point of view. This skill is especially important for teamwork, and is often emphasized in discussions of equality and inclusiveness in the workplace. Don't just listen, listen *attentively* to understand what the other person believes and wants. Meet them where they are, not where you think they should be. Understanding the other person's point of view can help you be a better, more effective person.

Did you make an effort to understand another's point of view today? Yes, or No?

Smile, and Mean It

"Smile in the mirror. Do that every morning and you'll start to see a big difference in your life." – Yoko Ono

There is a saying that goes something like, "do not open the door to your shop unless you are prepared to smile". In a recent *Psychology Today* blog, Sarah Stevenson summarizes scientific research which reports that smiling makes you and your body feel better by releasing dopamine, endorphins, and serotonin, sometimes called "the pleasure neurotransmitters".

Could a smile make you look better? Possibly. There is research that suggests that smiling faces are judged as more attractive than those that aren't smiling.

Could your smile make other people feel better? Again, it appears possible. Stevenson quotes research showing that "the part of your brain that is responsible for your facial expression of smiling when happy or mimicking another's smile resides in the Cingulate cortex, an unconscious, automatic response area". In a Swedish study, subjects were shown pictures of several emotions: joy, anger, fear, and surprise. When the picture of someone smiling was presented, the researchers asked the subjects to frown. Instead, they found that the facial expressions went directly to imitation of what subjects saw. It took conscious effort to "turn that smile upside down". So, if you're smiling at someone, it's likely they can't help but smile back. If they don't, they're making a conscious effort not to.

Some people seem to always have a smile on their face, while others may find it difficult to smile—or, more precisely, smile and mean it, feeling the positive emotions. Regardless of which applies to you, just try it. You can practice in a mirror. Be mindful that a smile shows readiness to interact positively and productively.

Did you smile at the beginning of every interaction today? Yes, or No?

Do Your Best Work

> *"Always do your best. What you plant now,*
> *you will harvest later." – Og Mandino*

Although this would seem to go without saying, success as a professional or as a student involves doing your best work. The PerfectCoaches snapshot asked when you do things best because it is important to know the triggers and rewards that bring out your best performance. This helps assure that you will develop pride in your work. Your inner craftsman encourages you to be proud of your craft. This means you should strive to have each thing you produce, be it a report or an analysis or performance on a test and be the best product you could offer.

> Knowing what times and circumstances influence you doing things best can help you perform better in all aspects.

In this context, mindfulness comes very close to the simple idea of paying attention to what you are doing. PerfectCoaches helps you understand when you do your best, and people often answer the question "*When* do I do it best?" by simply saying, "When I pay attention." Another way to say this is: I do my best work when I engage my brain.

Did you do your best today? Yes, or No?

Ask Questions and Try New Ideas

> *"The art and science of asking questions is the source*
> *of all knowledge." – Thomas Berger*

Our era is, perhaps more than any other, a time when it pays to think. A growing number of people, upwards of 50% of the workforce by some estimates, are *knowledge workers,* defined by Wikipedia as workers "whose main capital is knowledge". Typical examples may include, software engineers, physicians, pharmacists, architects, engineers, scientists, public accountants, lawyers, and academics, whose job is to think for a living.

In the information age where habits of thought have significant economic consequences, a trip to any library or bookstore will reveal shelves upon shelves of books on how to study, learn, and think. A Google search on the phrase "how to think better" produced almost 1.5 billion results. This discussion is not only for people in the knowledge work business, but it is also for *knowledge work professionals,* the word "professional" conveying the idea that the person has acquired the specific skills required for success.

Not only students, the world's apprentice knowledge workers, but highly accomplished professionals with mature careers usually acknowledge that they are always trying to improve how they approach problems and gather information. They are paid to think and create, and they want to keep getting better at it.

However, if you are a person who truly believes you are as successful as you will ever be, if you truly believe there is really no room for improvement in your intellectual skills, stop here. Skip this discussion.

Throughout history there have been thinkers who truly believed they were endowed with greatness, and there are students and software engineers today who truly believe they have a natural gift for comprehending problems effortlessly. If you think you have a gift and improvement is not only unnecessary but impossible, stop here.

> "The key to powerful thinking is powerful questioning. When we ask the right questions, we succeed as a thinker, for questions are the force that powers our thinking."
> –CriticalThinking.org

If you want to improve but are comfortable "just letting it happen" more or less randomly, as a by-product of your daily life, you can also stop here, because PerfectCoaches is not about leaving things to chance. Rather, it is a process that enables everyone to set goals for what they want to accomplish intellectually and improve their capacity to meet those goals in an organized way.

Asking questions can be great fun. Observe any toddler at play, and you'll see the raw energy that stems from curiosity. Then, of course, once that toddler begins to speak, there is the one question that never goes away: *Why*? Our brains create curiosity because they are designed to enable us to thrive in our environment.

Curiosity is expected of a child, though it can sometimes annoy the adults who deal with it. Rudyard Kipling's *The Elephant's Child*, referenced earlier, is an endearing tale of a young elephant who asked question after question.

In the life of mature human beings, forces in our daily routines and the culture itself tend to stifle our natural curiosity. Overcoming these forces is important. Curiosity is a gift, perhaps even a right. Indulge it. Ask yourself how and why things happen.

> Ask **Why** and **What If** throughout the day. These questions create new ideas and new opportunities.

Not only is curiosity the first virtue of a scientist, but it is also the first virtue of an effective member of a complex society. Adopt asking "why?" as a best-practice. Ask why often, at least once a day. Whenever possible, try to find the answer. Your brain will be happier, and you will be amazed at how many opportunities and solutions will show up in your life and work.

Be creative. Don't be afraid to ask the question "What if?" Not only that, try the new ideas that result. As most discussions of leadership emphasize, success often involves some sort of change and innovation. A best practice, even in day-to-day problem-solving, is to overcome the fear of trying a new way to do something. Sure, it may not work. But suppose it does? You've made the world work just a little bit better.

Asking questions is the gateway to creativity, innovation, and trying new ideas. Innovation is all around us. In many, perhaps all instances, breakthroughs take place because individuals and their teams are creative, ask questions, and try new ideas.

The biographies of great inventors reveal that each knew how to ask the right questions and find creative answers. Craig Venter's book, *A Life Decoded*, which deals with his personal role in the sequencing of the human genome, is a dramatic recent telling of the tale. The stories of Thomas Edison, Alexander Graham Bell, Marie Curie, the

Wright Brothers, and many others, show how innovation happens because someone was not afraid to try something new.

Did you ask questions and try something new today? Yes, or No?

Revel in Routine

> *"Habit is thus the enormous flywheel of society."*
> *- William James*

Getting into consistent habits about where and when you do things—eat, sleep, exercise, study, and complete tasks—is almost always beneficial. Whether you are in school, completing an assignment for your job, exercising, or just learning a subject because you want to, make it easy on yourself by finding a consistent time and place where the cues and reinforcers operating in the setting make you most productive. Enjoy your routine. Revel in it!

Students have homework, i.e., assignments completed outside of class. Throughout their career, professionals bring work home. In both instances, a routine time and place for getting it done, with predictable cues and reinforcements, is beneficial. If you are in school, study regularly throughout the semester for as many classes as you can. Some people study every day, others put it off to once or twice a week. In general, the more often the better, especially if it is at a regular time and place. Professionals should avoid last-minute preparation, i.e., "cramming", whenever possible.

Similarly, schedule your fitness activities, and keep to this schedule as you would to planned social occasions, business meetings, and classes. If you get used to working out before work or walking during your lunch hour, you're more likely to stick with it. Establishing a regular time and place generally makes learning new habits, and sticking with, them easier because the various cues and rewards that come from the environment are there consistently.

Once you establish a routine, it becomes possible to work with others who have a similar routine. Depending on the particulars, you can "work as a team". You may run with a co-worker over lunch or find a workout partner. If you're at the gym at the same time every day, look for people that may have similar goals.

Did you establish a routine today? Yes, or No?

Rehearse and Practice

> *"Practice makes perfect. After a long time of practicing, our work becomes natural, skillful, swift, and steady."*
> *– Bruce Lee*

When tasked to give a presentation, to one or many, at work or in school, rehearse it until you feel that one more rehearsal will not improve the product. The word "rehearse", which means "practice (a play, piece of music, or other work) for later public performance" is used to emphasize the importance of practicing. If you were going to perform in a play, you probably wouldn't want to face the audience without rehearsing until you were confident you knew your lines. Tests and presentations are performances, often with much more at stake than saying one's lines correctly in a play.

The old adage "practice makes perfect" is true throughout life, as every business consultant who thrives on "dry runs" for client presentations can attest. These dry runs usually involve testing answers to tough client questions. Students can practice alone by taking practice exams. In both cases, it is like an actor rehearsing his or her lines.

Some people enjoy reviewing their materials with a small group of friends, colleagues, or classmates. It is useful because they can work as a team—that is, have a sense of shared purpose and the goal of combined success.

Different formats work for different groups and different purposes. Professionals can review materials together in a "group read" format, meaning that even if materials were distributed in advance, the group goes through them end-to-end, together. Among college students, groups can work through chapters together, quizzing one another as they go along. Another technique is to compare class notes, ensuring they haven't missed any critical points.

Did you rehearse and practice something important today? Yes, or No?

Set a Pace to Do What is Required and Expected

"Make use of time, let not advantage slip."
– William Shakespeare

Preparation and planning are important for professional success, and it is useful to acquire the right habits in school. It is possible to view preparation, studying in particular, as boring, or tedious, or not worth the effort. It is also possible to view it as a useful and rewarding way to reach a goal, which is better. If you create rewards to help reinforce what you're doing, you can learn to pace yourself. For example, instead of working as an individual or a team for non-stop all afternoon, decide in advance on the timing of "logical" breaks.

College courses and professional education involves predefined expectations and requirements, but that is also true in other instances.

> Preparation and planning are vital tools for success.

Suppose you've decided to study how to brew beer at home. You are doing it on your own, but there are still expectations. The Brew-Your-Own Brewmeister really expects you to have the right equipment, perform steps in the right order, acquire the best ingredients, and so forth. Meeting the Brewmeister's expectations is the key to success in brewing your own beer.

The same is true when you're taking a class at a university, taking a class for personal development, or something else where you will be graded on meeting the expectations of the course. In professional life, managers and customers have expectations that need to be met. Professors and teachers have expectations too, and it is worth it to spend time making sure you understand them.

No matter what the course content or learning environment, if there is a classroom involved (including virtual classroom), pay attention and take note of what the instructor writes down or seems to think is important. Engage your brain. The same is true at work when a manager or leader is presenting ideas and giving direction.

Take note and clarify expectations, as necessary. Make it as easy as possible to remember and meet them.

Did you set a pace and do what was required and expected today? Yes, or No?

Excellence For A Lifetime

Learn and Write for Pleasure

> *"Writing is an exploration. You start from nothing and learn as you go." – E.L Doctorow*

Compared to other species, human babies have a lot to learn in order to adapt and thrive at every stage of life. Studying in its various shapes and forms is a necessary task. It begins in the first years of school and continues through life in the form of professional re-certification, updating product knowledge, or simply keeping up with technology. In that sense, we are stuck with it, yet it is even more important to realize that studying is something that your brain is designed to do. It's something that can be enjoyed, especially when it's done in an orderly way.

> Learning is a skill, and, perhaps more important, learning is part of life.

Be mindful that learning can and should be a pleasure. Take notes, either the traditional way on paper, or using a phone or other device to record key ideas. This is true when you study for a course or for any other reason, whether you are in college or learning material for professional development.

Learning is a skill, and, perhaps more important, learning is part of life. Embrace the need for it, cultivate the ability to do it well. As deadlines approach, keep a to-do list of specific things that need to get done. Avoid panic. Do that to-do list. This is especially important when a formal test is involved, but it is also important in professional life when you are preparing a formal presentation or even a conversation with a client.

You are more likely to learn for pleasure each day if you also take the time to *write* for pleasure. This simple activity can be accomplished in many ways, even if it's a small note to someone you know or to yourself.

Professionals do a lot of writing as part of their jobs, as do students, but writing shouldn't be viewed as only a job. You can write for pleasure, whether it's fiction, notes on a trip, emails, tweets, or a journal. Good old-fashioned pencil and paper diaries are also useful for exercising your brain and creating self-awareness.

> Although reading is a crucial element of lifelong learning, writing is important too.

In *Notes from Underground*, the Russian writer Fyodor Dostoyevsky observed that, "for everyday needs, the average person's awareness is more than sufficient, and it is about half or a quarter of that of the unhappy nineteenth-century intellectual…" His sarcastic point is that self-awareness can be a burden—the average person doesn't seem to need it, and the intellectuals who do need it do not necessarily enjoy it.

Regularly writing thoughts down just for the sake of expressing them can make self-awareness a more enjoyable and productive pursuit. Plus, writing is good mental exercise, and even short Twitter tweets or Facebook entries have the added advantage of being shared with others. Writing is often more fun if it is done for others to read.

Did you learn or write something for pleasure today? Yes, or No?

Follow your Syllabus for Lifelong Learning

> *"Live as if you were to die tomorrow. Learn as if you were to live forever." – Mahatma Gandhi*

"Live and learn." It's an expression we often hear in connection with life's small setbacks. "I should have known better than buy a used DVD player for three dollars. Oh well, *live and learn.*"

Such an important insight shouldn't be relegated solely to humble everyday uses. Consider the famous phrase *Cogito Ergo Sum*. Translated, it means "I think, therefore I am". This formulation by René Descartes is a pillar of modern philosophy. In simple terms, it means, "I must exist, or how else could I be having this thought?"

In its elegant simplicity, *Cogito Ergo Sum* solved, for most philosophers, the age-old problem of proving we exist at all.

It is interesting to juxtapose thinking and existing the other way around: *I am; therefore, I think.* In its simplest terms, this means, "Because I live, I think." This, in turn, implies the more you are *thinking,* the more you are *living.* It implies that the act of thinking makes life more meaningful.

Learning requires thinking, and at this point it is useful to take stock concerning what it will mean to learn throughout your lifetime. In your apprenticeship as a student, you are required to learn a set of materials that others have defined for you. As a professional, the nature of your work determines what you need to learn at any given time.

Thinking, learning, even studying, should not be limited to what you are required to learn. It's possibly just as important to study what you *want* to learn—for fun, for personal development, or to be social. Whatever your reason, there is always the opportunity to be a lifelong learner. Not only that, the secret, in the view of many, is simple, and can be expressed in one single word: READ.

A case can be made that reading is not just important to you, it is important for society and civilization as a whole. As immortalized in Ray Bradbury's *Fahrenheit 451*, the story of a book-torching fireman enforcing a law banning books. Book burning has been a tactic of oppression used, in modern times, by Nazis and the Islamic State. The burning of the great Library of Alexandria, though shrouded in mystery, has long been a symbol of the importance of great works and the cost to civilization when those works are lost.

A similar case can be made that thinking in its own right is not just important for you as a person, but for you as a citizen. In a long radio speech to the

> When you read, regardless of what you are reading, you and your brain are in charge. You are controlling the pace. You are interacting with the ideas. Although you can learn from a video or a conversation, reading gives you active control of how you digest ideas.

people of America, the character John Galt in Ayn Rand's novel *Atlas Shrugged* says, "The choice is still open to be a human being, but the price is to start from scratch, to stand naked in the face of reality and, reversing a costly historical error, to declare: I am, therefore I'll think."

The 1950's vintage *Atlas Shrugged* is a rather dark novel. The John Galt character isn't alluding to the joy of thinking, as we are, but rather the cultural necessity for it. You don't have to accept the political views of Ayn Rand in order to see how the freedom and vitality of a society rests on the willingness, and the capacity, of its people to think.

Reading helps make thinking and learning happen, and if you want reading to be a major part of your lifelong learning experience, one easy way to get started is to pick a group of great books or great thinkers to master on your own. You can decide, for example, to master the key ideas in science, history, cooking, sports, or whatever interest you want to pursue as a lifelong learner.

If you like fiction, you can decide to read everything by Stephen King or Shakespeare or J. K. Rowling or Toni Morrison. If you like towering scholarly works, just three by Daniel Boorstin (*The Discoverers, The Creators,* and *The Seekers*) can keep you occupied perhaps for a lifetime and, importantly, introduce you to many potential Coaches.

To find not just books but also audio and video works, browse a local library, or bookstore, or an online source like Amazon.com. You can't judge a book by its cover, true, but there is no shame in pulling a book based on its cover and seeing if it appeals to you.

The Ten Most Read Books list can be used as one of many possible foundations for a self-selected "syllabus" of ideas and stories to explore as a lifelong learner. One nice thing about this list is that, in many cases, you can watch the movie as well as read the book.

Ten Most Read Books in the World for the Past Fifty Years

This list, from Criticalthinking.org, may or may not be valid by everybody's definition, but in a sense, it doesn't matter—it's just an interesting list of books from which to choose. Plus, many of the books are also portrayed in movies, as denoted by a check mark (√).

√ 1. *The Bible*, with 3.9 billion copies sold. This is the Christian scripture consisting of the Old and New Testament.

√ 2. *Quotations from the Works of Mao Tse-tung*, with 820 million copies sold. Also called the *Little Red Book*, it explains the Chinese Communist ideology.

√ 3. *Harry Potter* (J. K. Rowling), with 400 million copies sold. This is a series about the life and magical world of Harry Potter, a boy wizard.

√ 4. *Lord of the Rings* (J. R. R. Tolkien), with 103 million copies sold, is an ornate epic about a fantasy Middle Earth, the One Ring, and good versus evil.

√ 5. *The Alchemist* (Paulo Coelho), with 65 million copies sold, tells the story of a shepherd boy who wanders to Africa to find The Alchemist and the secret to a treasure.

√ 6. *The Da Vinci Code* (Dan Brown), with 57 million copies sold. This book entails a religious mystery about Christ's life and legacy, set in modern Paris.

_ 7. *Twilight—The Saga* (Stephanie Meyer), with 43 million copies read. This is a love story between Bella Swan and Edward Cullen, a centuries-old immortal vampire.

√ 8. *Gone with the Wind* (Margaret Mitchell), with 33 million copies sold. This novel about the Civil War won the Pulitzer Prize and the film adaptation won an Oscar.

_ 9. *Think and Grow Rich* (Napoleon Hill), with 30 million copies sold. This 1937 classic draws on the success formulas of Henry Ford, Alexander Graham Bell, Thomas Edison, Theodore Roosevelt, Wilbur Wright, and others.

√ 10. *Diary of a Young Girl* (Anne Frank), with 27 million copies sold, is a young girl's account of survival in Nazi-occupied Holland.

Although reading is a wonderful thing, the 21st century is a multi-media era with many other assets besides the written word. The value of the cinema as a learning venue cannot be ignored. Just as there are "top" book lists, there are top movie lists. For example, rottentomatoes.com offers the "Top 100 movies ever according to their Tomatometer Score". The score is "based on the published opinions of hundreds of film and television critics, a trusted measurement of movie and TV programming quality for millions of moviegoers".

As always, it is up to you to decide the validity of the claim. What's important, though, is that it is a list, a somewhat unusual one at that, to get you started.

RottenTomatoes.com Top 10 Movie List

1. The Wizard of Oz (1939)
2. The Third Man (1949)
3. Citizen Kane (1941)
4. All About Eve (1950)
5. The Cabinet of Dr. Caligari (1920)
6. A Hard Day's Night (1964)
7. Modern Times (1936)
8. The Godfather (1972)
9. E.T. The Extra-Terrestrial (1982)
10. Metropolis (1927)

You may also want to learn by experiencing places and events. Bucketlist.org offers many interesting ideas for lifelong learning, as does Patricia Schultz's book *1,000 Places to See Before You Die: A Traveler's Life List.* Why start a bucket list late in life like the Morgan Freeman and Jack Nicholson characters in *The Bucket List*? Start it and pursue it now.

Just as professors create a syllabus guides for a course, you can create one for your life, following and updating it as your tastes and interests change.

Have you followed your lifelong learning syllabus today? Yes, or No?

Chapter Five
Customer Engagement
and Persuasion

Sales and Customer Service are important professions because they ultimately determine the success of the business and, in fact, the entire economy. Every customer-facing professional is, to some degree, selling the company's products. In PerfectCoaches, the foundational skills, for these roles involves *persuasion*, i.e., influencing the thoughts and actions of others.

In sales, the goal is simple: persuade the customer to buy the product or idea. In customer service, whether in person or over the phone, the goal is more subtle: provide a level of service that persuades the customer that the company is committed to their satisfaction, now and in the future.

No matter where it happens, persuasion can be seen as a three-step process where you *Prepare*; *Present* the product; then *Persist* to close the sale. The Three Ps of Persuasion—Prepare, Present, Persist—is a simple model to follow as well as a convenient mental map for organizing specific techniques that work in each phase. Click the Lightbulb to learn more about each skill, then select one to master. Success comes with mastering them all and following the process every time.

This chapter is devoted to a special skillset consisting of habits and behaviors especially valuable for those in occupations that require you to shape the ideas and actions of others. This is designed for leadership, sales, and customer service. To the extent that most people use their persuasive skills in daily life, the foundational habits can be adapted and used by anyone.

Although leadership involves the broad competencies exhibited by the great leaders to be discussed later, to be an effective leader you need to understand the ideas you are presenting and what the people you hope to lead believe and want. Similarly, to be a successful sales professional, you need to understand the product or idea you are selling and the person, or people, you want to buy it.

In both cases the admonition to *know thyself* also applies. You need to know your strengths, your vulnerabilities, and the techniques that work best for you.

Leaders, sales professionals, and others can adopt the behaviors and skills within this skillset as they see fit. This discussion is not like the countless blogs, books, or seminars offering tips, suggestions, rules, and prescriptions that guarantee, in some sense or another, that you will become a highly effective leader or "hit the ball out of the park" in sales or customer service. Rather, it builds on the PerfectCoaches method to help you sift through the universe of ideas about persuasion in its many forms to find what works for you. The framework presented here can help you organize that search.

The Free Online Dictionary defines the word "sell" in several ways. One definition is, "To exchange or deliver for money or its equivalent." This is the classic meaning of a sale as a cash transaction. You give me cash, and in return I give you this piece of merchandise or render this service.

Another definition is, "To persuade another to recognize the worth or desirability of something," as in "They sold me on the idea." Selling ideas in their own right is challenging, and it is often the case that selling a product involves selling the ideas behind it.

Persuasion professionals must develop their ability to persuade in order to earn a livelihood. This includes salespeople of all sorts who broker an exchange of money for goods or services. But it also includes the much broader array of professionals—in management, customer service, law, medicine, entertainment, and politics—for whom selling ideas is a core competency. It is important to note that the word *professional* conveys the idea that the person has acquired the specific skills and professional habits needed for success.

There are also many customer service careers that require what are sometimes called "people skills." Here the goal is not necessarily persuading others to buy a product or idea, but rather to make interactions effective, efficient, and pleasant. These roles include retail salesclerks and cashiers which, according to the U.S. Bureau of

Labor Statistics, are the two largest occupations, making up as much as 10 percent of the U.S. labor force, depending on your definition. Occupations that require similar skills, such as administrative staff, customer service representative, and roles in the hospitality industry (e.g., food servers, bartenders) are also large and growing.

For these roles where people skills help "sell" the customer on the value of the overall experience with a company, the term "people professionals" may be a better fit. The Skillset Resumes for both careers are similar, and we use these two terms interchangeably. In addition, every customer-facing role is subject to what is discussed later as "The Sam Walton Test".

If you are a sales professional who truly believes you are as successful as you will ever be, if you truly believe there is really no room for improvement in your "powers of persuasion", stop here. You don't need to read this chapter.

Throughout history there have been leaders who truly believed they were endowed with greatness, and there are people in sales today, who truly believe they have a natural gift for selling. If you think you are a truly gifted communicator and improvement is not only unnecessary but impossible, stop here.

If you want to improve but are comfortable letting it happen serendipitously, you can also stop here, because PerfectCoaches is not about being lucky or leaving things to chance. Rather, it is a process that enables everyone to set goals for what they want to accomplish professionally and improve their capacity to meet those goals in an organized way.

A lot of sales, leadership, and customer service training consists of an audience of professionals watching a speaker tell them what they should do. For the most part, the listener is passive. PerfectCoaches makes passive participation impossible. It does not rattle off a lot of sales tips. This book does not tell you, for example, to follow up with customers. It does not tell you to listen better. Rather, it challenges you to ask yourself "How can I follow up more effectively?" and "How can I listen better?"

Successful leaders, salespeople, and customer service professionals are mindful of the fact that they are often performing spontaneously in real time, adapting their tactics to real situations. This is where the PerfectCoaches commitment to simplicity and discipline is particularly useful.

Our approach to the habits of persuasion uses the "rule of three", based on the idea that people tend to remember three things presented as a list of ideas or things that go together. Using this rule is a useful habit in its own right. Consider these well-known examples:

> Good, better, best.
> Going, going, gone.
> Friends, Romans, countrymen.
> Blood, sweat, and tears.
> Father, Son, and Holy Spirit.
> Faith, hope, and charity.
> Stop, look, and listen.
> The good, the bad, and the ugly.
> Life, liberty, and the pursuit of happiness.
> Government of the people, by the people, for the people.

Let's add another commonly used device: top-10 lists. Lists of 10 things have been around since biblical times, with the Old Testament's list of Ten Commandments being perhaps the best known and most often cited. David Letterman enshrined top-10 lists in late night culture, and there is even a website, toptenz.net, devoted to the idea. Following our commitment to simplicity, this skillset for perfecting persuasion offers a top-10 list of rules of three. This stack can be the heart of your Skillset Résumé as a persuasion or service professional.

Follow the "Three Ps of Persuasion": Prepare, Present, Persist

> *"There are no secrets to success. It is the result of preparation, hard work, and learning from failure."*
> *– Colin Powell*

The first principle is to apply the three Ps of persuasion. Persuasion is a process. You perfect it. The word perfect is not just an adjective to describe The Coaches, it's a verb that describes what you are trying to do. You are learning to perfect the process of persuasion.

Whether you are a leader getting ready to address a group or meet with a stakeholder you need to influence, or you are an "inside sales" professional greeting a customer walking into your store, or you are an "outside sales" professional entering the office or store of your customer, success can rest on a simple list of habits.

Many leaders and speakers or salespeople focus nearly all of their attention on the persuasive encounter, that is, a speech, a presentation, or a sales pitch. The three Ps of persuasion are a reminder that preparation and persistent follow up are often just as important, or in some cases more important, than the presentation itself. Within each phase—*preparing, presenting, persisting*—there are three lists of three, as illustrated below.

A Skillset for Customer Service

Follow the Three Ps of Persuasion: Prepare, Present, Persist and their accompanying acronyms:

Prepare

Always Be Confident
Always Be Charming
Always Think YES (Your Elevator Speeches)

Present

Always Be Curious
Always Bring Choices
Always Be Closing

Persist

Always Follow Up
Always Open Doors
GPS: Grow, Perfect, Succeed

Prepare

Not only do you prepare for a specific meeting, leadership presentation, or sales encounter, you are constantly preparing yourself for *success*. The best practices for teamwork and learning discussed in Chapter Four apply throughout the careers of people at every level. They can be thought of as the basic components of a Skillset Résumé for you as a professional, and following those best practices is basically the first step in the preparation process.

If you are a leader, not only are these best practices candidates for your personal Skillset Résumé, but you can also lead by example and provide the same goals to everyone in your organization. That overall professional readiness manifests itself in the confidence and, yes, charm, you exhibit in persuasive encounters.

Always Be Confident

> *"Optimism is the faith that leads to achievement. Nothing can be done without hope and confidence." – Hellen Keller*

Many professionals consider themselves very confident. Others will say they feel a lack of confidence. It is better to think of confidence, not as a trait you were born with or acquired earlier in life, but *rather the sense you have, at this moment, that you are ready to succeed.*

Product knowledge is often the main ingredient creating confidence in a salesperson. No matter how many products there are, no matter how simple or complex they may be, knowing how each product works and, most important of all, how they fulfill a particular customer need, will boost confidence.

Knowing what your products are and what each one does is crucial for every form of knowledge work. Confidence in persuasion comes not only from knowing your product(s), but also knowing your customers or audience, and, of course, knowing yourself. You build confidence as part of preparation, then demonstrate it when you present. Make eye contact. Speak deliberately, being mindful of how your words are received. Exude confidence that your product knowledge is wide and deep enough to answer questions, overcome objections, and explain the product fully when the time comes.

If done correctly, practice produces confidence. If you were going to perform in a play, you probably wouldn't want to walk on stage without rehearsing first. Tests and presentations are performances too, often with much more at stake than looking prepared in a play. We are really talking about practice. The age-old adage, "practice makes perfect," is true throughout life, as every business consultant who thrives on "dry runs" for client presentations can attest.

You also build confidence by setting the stage, as, for example, in this set of ideas for outside sales:

- Arrive early.
- Review the buyer's personal information and the notes from the last sale. This information should be listed on the account card. Plan your warmup.
- Review your objective and pre-written plan.
- Check up from the neck up! Looking good? Got everything?
- Take a quick visual inventory.
- Greet the buyer, conduct a quick warm up and excuse yourself to conduct an inventory. While taking an inventory be sure to re-merchandise and straighten. If applicable, use inventory control sheets to log product counts and make notes.
- Pre-write reorders.
- After conducting the inventory, walk the store looking for new opportunities. Look for space to establish presentation real estate.
- Formulate a master plan. What to show first, what concepts to emphasize.
- Establish an "I'm okay, you're okay" relationship. Take as much time as needed to get your customer ready to move into a selling/buying situation.
- Solid preparation means an established rhythm and routine of your day, week, and month. A well-planned, well-understood routine builds confidence.

Depending on the context you are working in, there are some basic concepts that nearly always apply:

Pre-plan: fail to plan, plan to fail. Plan your call cycle, plan your week, plan your day, and plan your sale, and you will succeed.

Be ready with samples and demonstrations: always bring them with you because you never know where the presentation may go. Even if you are selling software, be ready to do a quick demo if the situation warrants it.

Present the entire selection: don't prejudge. Take inventory and ask for reorders first. Then move into presenting everyday goods (both old and new) before presenting seasonal products. It is not about what is new, it is about what retails.

"Oh, by the way": always have an item/concept to present to the buyer once the sale is complete. Presenting a product at the end of your presentation often works, as the buyer may be more receptive once they believe the sale is over.

Always Be Charming

"It is absurd to divide people into good and bad.
People are either charming or tedious." – Oscar Wilde

You are not just presenting a product or solution; you are presenting yourself. The audience is more likely to like your *product* if they like *you*.

Some people resist the idea that charm fosters success, and also resist the idea that you actually prepare to be charming. The dictionary defines charming as *"Fascinating or delightful; very likable."* This can be a tall order even for those who believe that they are charming by nature. It might seem impossible for those who do not see themselves as a likable person and think, somehow, fate meant for it to be that way.

Although by definition charm is in the eye of the beholder, charm is a set of behaviors, a way of presenting yourself, that you can master if you think it will improve your effectiveness. You can make charm part of your personal brand. Although a visit to a nursery full of newborns might lead you to believe that some kids are born more charming than others, if you could fast-forward into their lives, you would see that many of the charming behaviors they exhibit as adults are learned.

That Barbizon Modeling and many local "charm schools" have served multiple generations in their community is a testament to the idea that charm can be learned. They teach etiquette, poise, speaking skills, and many of the best practices for work, learning, and life discussed earlier. They encourage students to cultivate their most attractive traits, and, perhaps most important, to "put your best self forward" in every situation.

Although some people might prefer another phrase, say, "Always be courteous," there is no shame in wanting to be charming. It simply means that you are prepared to present your best self when it comes time to present your product or idea. If you believe appearances count, do a "check up from the neck up" to be sure your physical presentation projects the right image. Be likable and interesting. Pay compliments. Ultimately, the package your customer buys includes your product, you, and your company.

Always Think YES (Your Elevator Speeches)

"If you can't explain it simply, you don't understand it well enough." – Albert Einstein

Your elevator speech explains you and what you offer. Effective leaders and salespeople who are truly immersed in their craft are constantly planning and re-thinking their elevator speech, going so far as to rehearse it and other parts of their presentation in front of a mirror. This 20- to 30-second "pitch", brief enough to be recited on a short elevator ride, presents a problem and how your product (or idea) solves that problem. For example, here is an elevator pitch for PerfectCoaches:

Companies, universities, and leadership coaches use PerfectCoaches to help people learn new habits and skills and then practice them continuously.

Twenty words, 15 seconds. A good elevator speech delivers a *veto-proof message.* Nobody can disagree that the implied problem (people need to learn new skills and habits) exists and that your product will solve it.

Note the term "elevator speeches" (plural), not "elevator speech", because perfecting the persuasion process means having multiple elevator speeches at the ready. There is the main pitch, or speech, about the product, but you will usually end up using an elevator speech about the company more generally, and a speech about you. People begin by focusing on the product or idea you are presenting, but they will want to know about the company, and at least a bit about you, so be ready.

The important thing about YES is not that it's an acronym for Your Elevator Speech, but rather that it is what you want your customer to say when you are ready to close the deal.

Always give your elevator speech as soon as you think the customer is ready, whether the customer asks for it or not, no matter what course the conversation takes. Some persuasive encounters move fast. Some meander. No matter which is true, give your quick pitch as soon as possible. Never let a conversation end without presenting the basic pitch for your product.

Present

Now we come to the second phase of the persuasion process, the "persuasive encounter" itself. This is where you present the idea or product and persuade someone to buy it. You let the customer do most of the talking. Your role is surprisingly straightforward. You ask questions. You discuss the choices and options available to the customer. Finally, you close the encounter. All the while, you have been closing the deal. Always be closing!

You must totally control this process while making sure the customer believes they are controlling it, because they are. This may seem paradoxical, but the fact is, an effective persuasion professional takes responsibility for the process, but the customer is responsible for the outcome.

Always Be Curious

"Questions beget answers. Answers beget understanding.
Understanding gets you the sale." – Anonymous

A useful rule of thumb for persuasive presentations is that you should listen twice as much as you speak. A compliment coupled with a question is a good way to start. The compliment gives the customer an opportunity to talk about themselves. It also establishes a dialog versus a monologue which is one of the most frequent mistakes salespeople make: talking too much. The sample creates the emotion. The choices give the other person a chance to say yes. When you ask a yes or no question, there's nowhere to go when they say no. Create choices that give a client a chance to say yes, and the chance of success goes up dramatically. For example:

- Ask open-ended questions about the buyer's goals. "Tell me about…"
- Recognize that the first question a buyer asks is a buying signal.
- Close page-by-page and concept-by-concept.
- Sell the product line completely.
- Listen and overcome major objections, dismissing minor ones. Objections represent a request for more information. Agree with them and say "Yes, I understand how you feel, we hear that sometimes from customers," and then overcome that particular objection.

To emphasize a point made earlier, while curiosity is expected of a child, it can sometimes annoy adults. Again, Rudyard Kipling's The *Elephant's Child* is an endearing story on that very subject.

In the life of mature human beings, forces in our daily routines and the culture itself tend to stifle our natural curiosity. Overcoming these forces is important. Curiosity is a gift, perhaps even a right. Indulge it. Ask yourself how and why things happen.

Not only is curiosity the first virtue of a scientist, but it is also the first virtue of a citizen of the earth. Adopt asking "why?" as a best-practice. Ask "why?" often, at least once a day. And make it a habit to try to find the answer. Your brain will be happier, and you will be amazed at how many opportunities and solutions will show up in your life and work.

Keep asking questions. Use emotional intelligence to know when the customer wants to move on. Listen much more than you talk. You know your product, and now you are learning about their problem.

Ask questions to determine the buyer's wants, needs, and goals. Use "Tell me about" questions frequently. "Tell me about the problems you are having with…?" All questions should be open-ended.

Avoid closed questions that result in a "Yes" or "No" response. When marketing to a retailer, walk the customer to the sales floor during the discussion. Take the customer out of their element and bring them into yours.

Always Bring Choices

> *"The customer's choice should not be to buy or not.*
> *It should be good, better, or best." – Anonymous*

When presenting your product or idea, the customer's choice should never be whether or not to buy; rather, it should be which variation of your product they want, and how much. Ask the customer to buy more than the minimum whenever appropriate. Use positive alternative closes, such as "Would you like six or twelve?" to upsell the customer on your better retailing products. Try these options as well:

- If the choice is between two or more versions of your product, ask "Which of our books would you like?" "Which testing/contract option appeals most?"
- Present alternative choices as a way to close. "Would you like six or twelve styles, or all twelve? Which would you prefer?"
- Show your best "Yes" item, or concept, first. Start the presentation with a "yes."
- Use testimonials and stories to reinforce the power of your product.
- Always start BIG.
- Ask questions throughout the selling sequence.
- Use words like "us", "we", and "our", throughout the presentation, reinforcing a partnership.

Always Be Closing

> *"A-B-C. A—Always. B—Be. C—Closing. Always.*
> *Be. Closing. Always be closing!"* – Alec Baldwin,
> *Glengarry Glen Ross*

This best-practice, discussed earlier in the book, deserves special mention here. The term "closing" comes from the world of sales. It is the final step in a real estate transaction, but, more generally, it is the point at which the customer agrees to make a purchase. Closing can mean making a sale, or it may mean setting a time for a follow-on discussion.

The Alec Baldwin character in *Glengarry Glen Ross* has one valid point, which is that success in sales requires a constant mindfulness of the ultimate goal, which is to close the deal. Even when you are paying compliments, being charming, or simply listening to the customer, remain mindful that your goal is a successful close.

As you ask questions and present choices you begin to perform what are called *trial closes* in which you assess the customer's readiness to buy by asking for an opinion about your product. If the customer has decided already he or she will tell you, but you do not ask for a decision. Rather, again, these are open-ended questions designed to identify and overcome objections while learning more about customer needs and preferences. You can ask:

- What are your thoughts on this product (or idea)?
- Which of these features seems most useful for you right now, or perhaps in the future?
- When do you think you would want this product or service?
- What do you think is your next step?

As you ask these questions, use emotional intelligence to pay attention to the customer's body language and facial expressions, not just their words. There are certain techniques, tricks of the trade, so to speak, that can help you do this. Here are some examples.

First, there is the "input mode only" technique. After asking a question, try to not talk at all. This may be difficult for you, and you want to be sure that it doesn't create awkward moments in the encounter, but just try waiting until the other person signals that they want *you* to say something. By saying less and hearing more, you can target the remarks you do make on the concerns and interests of the customer. This is sometimes called "shut up to sell."

Another technique is "thought ballooning." As you begin your trial closes, the customer may say one thing, but emotional intelligence (or gut instinct, if you prefer) tells you they are thinking something else. You can use your emotional intelligence to anticipate sales resistance better if you draw an imaginary "thought balloon" over their head—like the ones in comic books—and fill in what you believe they're really thinking.

A similar technique is "the stop light test." To bring focus to your observation of the other person, imagine a traffic light on their forehead. When the light is green, keep focused on that line of thought. When it's flashing amber, slow down and be cautious. When it's red, it means you should stop—try something else or maybe just close the encounter and move on.

And finally, when presenting to a group, there is a temptation to focus on the formal leader versus the other people who need to be persuaded. The formal leader is important, but it is also necessary to get a quick read on the relationships among the people present and a rough idea of what each person is like. Here, the "10th-grade test" can be useful.

Like thought ballooning, the 10th-grade test involves guesswork. In this case you are guessing what each person was like in the 10th grade, a point at which their true personalities and intentions were more likely to be on display. The 10th-grade test can help you more quickly identify types, by whatever labels you like to use. Here's one example:

> Teacher (formal leader)
> Teacher's pet (key influencer/proxy decision maker)
> Brown-nose ("yes" man or woman)
> Bully (I-want-my-way conversation dominator)
> Brat (active naysayer)
> Bored (Passive naysayer)
> Brainiac (asks best questions, influential)
> Class clown (jokes can reveal group dynamic issues)

Although there can be a slap-stick element to it, the 10th-grade test, like thought ballooning, can be a useful exercise in emotional intelligence. You are challenging yourself to predict the group dynamics, issues, and roles of the customer's team by quickly assessing their enduring personalities based on a brief encounter.

Eventually, you know whether you closed the deal because you ask for a decision from the buyer. Along the way, persuasion in every face-to-face setting—sales, management, leadership, customer service—requires reading cues in a person's body language and facial expressions. It's about knowing when you should move on to another point or give up entirely. Begin trying these techniques, keeping track of the results in your journal.

Persist

Sales professionals are sometimes criticized for being "too persistent", i.e., pesky in some annoying way. The stereotypes of used car salesmen or telemarketers come to mind.

Yet, look up the definition of "persist" on Google, and you will encounter a more noble definition of the term: *to continue firmly or obstinately in an opinion or a course of action in spite of difficulty, opposition, or failure.* Just as noble are the word's Latin origins in *persistere*, from *per-* (thorough, steadfastly) and *sistere* (to stand). Thus, to persist is to stand, and continue, steadfastly.

The great leaders discussed later in the book were persistent in this original sense. They kept at it, overcoming obstacles and disappointment. If you are mindful of an obligation to take the needs of others into account, persistence is not only a useful habit, but also an admirable quality. Particularly for sales professionals, it involves follow up, moving forward after failure, and a commitment to growth and success.

Always Follow Up

> *"Not following up with your prospects is the same as filling up your bathtub without first putting the stopper in the drain." – Michelle Moore*

There is a lot of research on effective sales, and there are many, many "rules of thumb" that offer advice about how to succeed. Writers and researchers are, however, nearly unanimous in the view that effective follow up is essential. Here is a basically undisputed principle: it often takes multiple follow up "touches", whether they are emails or phone calls or personal visits, to close a deal with a client.

It is unusual for a prospective client to make a major purchase decision after your first conversation with them, or even the second. It may take multiple contacts, possibly with multiple people within an organization before that initial presentation is converted to a sale or a contract. Some sales organizations use the rule of thumb that five to seven touches are needed to close a sale. Following that guideline, you would contact the client at least five times before determining whether they are going to buy.

You simply must follow up. The plan for follow up begins the moment the presentation is complete. Experienced leaders often delegate elements of the follow up to others. Sales professionals often do it themselves, but sometimes the organization provides resources specifically to help with follow up (and also, in some cases, preparing).

The phrase "always follow up" lacks the power of "always be closing", but the habit is just as crucial for success. In many, perhaps most, leadership and sales situations, much of the hard work remains to be done after the presentation. To succeed in the persuasion business, you must always follow up. Examples of follow up include:

- Setting up the next meeting(s);
- Getting back to answer questions;
- Asking for referrals; and
- Following up to check on customer satisfaction.

When possible, follow up should be presented to the customer (or audience, in the case of leaders) as a display of interest, part of the charm of the presenter.

It is rare that a person or audience is persuaded the first time they hear an idea presented or see a product. For that reason, effective, well-planned follow up is an essential ingredient for an organization's sales program. It is crucial in all forms of persuasion.

In the case of customer service, the "Three S Rule of Service" is a compact, easily repeated version of the "Three Ps of Persuasion" that can be used in every interaction with a customer. The Three S Rule consists of three steps:

First, **Smile** and greet the customer. This *prepares* you and the customer for a successful interaction.

Second, **Stop** what you were doing if the customer has a request or appears to need service. Give the customer your undivided attention. Here you *present* yourself to the customer as a resource.

Third, **See** to it that the customer is satisfied. You and your team must *persist* until the customer need is met. Here, your product knowledge is important, but it is also important that you know when to pass the customer's request to another responsible person on your team. Customer service is a team effort.

There are many guidelines for good customer service, and most can be seen through the lens of the Three S Rule. Dr. Al Infande at *Selfgrowth.com* makes several valid points. He believes the customer is the most important person in your business (because without customers your business would not exist). He is also a big proponent of good first impressions, because his research says that it takes six good impressions to overcome one negative impression.

Dr. Infande also believes in several tenets of good customer service:

- Treat the customer the same way you would expect to be treated.
- As best you can, anticipate and accommodate their needs.
- Create a "home" environment by being courteous, gracious, and grateful.
- Deliver value for the customer's money.
- How you resolve complaints will make a difference in whether that customer returns.
- Go the extra mile with service.
- Make eye contact, smile, and show you care about them and their business.
- Arguing with the customer is never a good idea.
- Handle all problems and transactions professionally.
- If you don't have the solution the customer needs, direct them to someone who does.

Most of these suggestions involve following up—persisting—until the customer need is met, while the rest of the list pertain more to preparation and presentation. What also makes this list useful is that it lends itself to the creation of a comprehensive stack of habits important for customer service professionals in a variety of retail, hospitality, and administrative settings.

Persuasion in leadership is a complex process specific to each issue and audience, but persistence is almost always a key ingredient for success. The book *Change Agents in Sunglasses: The Art and Science of Leadership in the Information Age* shows how this process works in organizations consisting of a complex mix of people, process, and technology.

First, a leader must develop a vision, *preparing* them to move a team, an organization, perhaps even a whole society, as in the case of leaders discussed earlier, forward.

The second phase, planning, involves *presenting* the vision to a widening circle of people involved. Here the leadership team refines the vision in what is, in effect, a series of trial closes where the message is tested and refined.

Persistence is absolutely necessary in the third phase, *implementing* the vision. A leader must move the vision through many steps and many audiences in order to make it happen.

Always Open Doors

> *"If opportunity doesn't knock, build a door."*
> *– Milton Berle*

PerfectCoaches invites you to accept the world as it is. Sales and leadership are all about dealing with, and responding to, rejection. In door-to-door magazine subscription sales, a rule of thumb was that you sold to one customer out of ten. You expected to hear "no" nine times for every "yes."

You can't really talk about sales or leadership without discussing disappointment, rejection, and setbacks. These are a given. How you handle them is the key to your success. Evaluating what went wrong and right is the key. Working on the missteps and building on the successes is key.

Above all else, close the rejection door and open the "new day door" with a smile at every opportunity.

You close the Rejection Door when you make the business decision that this customer is not going to buy this thing right now. They rejected your offer, at least for now, so it is time to close that door and politely move on.

You open the opportunity door by putting any negative feelings behind you and approaching the next customer positively. It is a fresh start.

You make it a Success Door by applying your best techniques, including a smile, to that next customer encounter.

> ## The Concept of the Three Doors
>
> - Close the Rejection Door
> - Open the Opportunity Door
> - Go in, smile, and make it a Success Door.

Grow, Perfect, Succeed

"Perfect is also a verb. It is what we do, not what we are." – Anonymous

To repeat what was said in the beginning, the PerfectCoaches process is built for you and belongs to you. You perfect the process by using it to grow and succeed. Hence the final rule of three is termed GPS for: *Grow, Perfect, Succeed.*

People use a GPS—Global Positioning System—to get places in their car. An onboard computer takes data from satellites above the planet and makes complex calculations, called trilateration, to identify the location of the vehicle.

Wouldn't life be great if it were as simple as telling your GPS where you want to go, not in your car, but in your life and career, and have a voice tell you exactly, step-by step, how to get there? You would get all the direction you need.

But life doesn't work that way. We must make the decisions that get us to life's personal and professional destination. Yes, we can get ideas from those around us but the decisions on what, when, where, and why we do something has to come from within. We use that powerful onboard computer, our brain, to make that happen. This brings us back to the very first best-practice discussed in the book—engage your brain.

Engaging our brain, we can use our syllabus for lifelong learning to know the greats like Sam Walton, or great ideas, like those in Og Mandino's book *The World's Greatest Salesman.* The PerfectCoaches thought experiment invites you to imagine working with them as your coach.

Sam Walton, founder of Walmart, was one of the great leaders in the history of retail. He famously said, "there is only one boss. The customer. And he can fire everybody in the company from the chairman on down, simply by spending his money somewhere else."

Walton's biography is a story about leadership in business. Born in Kingfisher, Oklahoma in 1918, he used a $25,000 loan from his father, a bank president, to open his first Ben Franklin store. Frustrated by the fact that Ben Franklin management did not want to pursue the rural market as aggressively as Walton wanted to, he founded his first Wal-Mart store in 1962.

Walton's deep understanding of the rural retail market was one of the keys to his success. He understood his customers and learned even more when he personally played the role of greeter in his stores. In the half century since, Walmart has grown to dominate the marketplace by building upon Walton's insight that people want the most variety and best quality at the best price.

Inside Walmart's price-driven business model, it is a challenge to also offer good customer service. Still, you know you have excelled when customers come back. Keeping customers spending their money with your business—let's call this passing the *Sam Walton Test*—is a test that every persuasion professional must pass every day.

Every interaction with a customer is ultimately about one behavior you are trying to influence, namely, keeping that person's business. Every customer-facing employee is in the persuasion business because it is their job to influence the customer to buy today and return to buy again.

Indeed, the ubiquitous nature of the "Sam Walton Test", or "Sam Walton Imperative", is what makes it crucial for every business to have its customer-facing staff acquire the foundational skills and best practices of Persuasion Professionals.

Alongside the accomplishments of people like Sam Walton, you can consider the writings of Og Mandino. Although Augustine "Og"

Mandino is not particularly well-known outside of the world of sales and motivational writing, his bestselling book *The Greatest Salesman in the World* is regarded as a classic, and his books have sold over 50 million copies.

Drawing on his own experience with disappointment and the need to persist, Mandino addressed a life in sales, and life in general, in an almost spiritual sense. *The Greatest Salesman in the World* opens with the words "I will persist until I succeed." The following quotes explain the challenges of selling.

> *The career I have chosen is laden with opportunity, yet it is fraught with heartbreak and despair and the bodies of those who have failed, were they piled one atop another, would cast its shadow down upon all the pyramids of the earth.*

> *Never has there been a map, however carefully executed to detail and scale, which carried its owner over even one inch of ground... Action, alone, is the tinder which ignites the map... my dreams, my plans, my goals, into a living force. Action is the food and drink which will nourish my success. I will act now.*

His ideas are organized around what he called the Ten Scrolls, several of which are consistent with the PerfectCoaches concept. Of specific interest is *The Scroll Marked VIII: Today I will multiply my value a hundredfold.* Here Mandino writes:

> *I will be as my own prophet and though all may laugh at my utterances, they will hear my plans, they will know my dreams; and thus, there will be no escape for me until my words become accomplished deeds. Today I will multiply my value a hundredfold.*

Mandino's several books emphasized that turning words into accomplished deeds means doing things and making things happen. That is what PerfectCoaches is all about.

Given the spiritual dimension in Mandino's work and the writing of other authors cited in this book, it is worth noting that your core self, the animating force in your day-to-day life, is somewhat akin to the concept of a *soul,* which Merriam Webster defines as "the immaterial essence, animating principle, or actuating cause of an individual life."

Although the PerfectCoaches concept of core self does not imply the existence of an immortal soul in a religious sense, the PerfectCoaches emphasis on self-awareness can help in the search for purpose in life. To answer the question, "where am I going?" is to begin to discover meaning and purpose in your life.

PerfectCoaches can be useful to anyone of any faith, or no faith at all. Yet, interestingly, it would be possible to use PerfectCoaches as a way to master basic habits endorsed by religions and philosophies. Examples include the Ten Commandments of the Old Testament, Christ's Sermon on the Mount, the Five Pillars of Islam, Buddha's Eight-fold Path, The Ten Disciplines of Hinduism, even the admonitions contained in the eighty-one verses of Lao-Tso's *Tao Tee Ching.* To the extent that these teachings suggest things you should *do,* they are habits that can be mastered.

Also—and spoiler alert—Og Mandino's greatest salesman in the world turns out to be Paul of Tarsus, Saint Paul of the Christian New Testament.

Chapter Six
Live Well: Thank Your Body

Living well is a matter of habit. The next two best practices, or more precisely stacks of best practices, involve *thanking your body* and *thanking life*. These are presented as skillsets, i.e., lists of specific behaviors that are learned individually but practiced together to achieve a single goal.

Just as you can think of the work and learning skills discussed thus far as part of your *Skillset Résumé*, you can think of these as your *Wellness Résumé*. You may even prefer the broader concept of a *Life Skills Résumé* that could include not just wellness behaviors, but also selected skills for work and learning.

Thank Your Body

Success in work and learning is easier to achieve, and to enjoy, if you feel good. "When you have your health, you have everything." We hear that saying a lot. But how often do we hear, "When you don't have your health, you have nothing." Not very often. That's as it should be. For the countless people struggling with health issues—whether they know it or not—it would be wrong to discount the many other things they have in their life.

Yet it would be fair to say that, when you have your health, all the other things you have can be worth so much more. That's what *high-level wellness* is all about. It is a way to get there. It helps you see nutrition, fitness, and medicine in the context of the complete life you lead. It begins with self-awareness and continues as an ongoing process of improving one's health, nutrition, and fitness one behavior at a time.

High-level wellness emphasizes the integration of body, mind, spirit, and the habits of daily life to maximize the enjoyment and vitality that simply being alive offers each of us. And, importantly, companies and universities achieve better performance when the "whole person" who reports for work or comes to class, is a healthy and well-balanced individual.

Thanking your body and thanking life are paths to achieving high-level wellness. In his book, *High-Level Wellness*, Halbert Dunn calls wellness "an integrated method of functioning which is oriented toward maximizing the potential of which the individual is capable of functioning within the environment."

Dunn's research helped give him a holistic view of wellness that went beyond his medical training. He believed wellness is not just the absence of disease in a medical sense, but rather it is an approach that encompasses proper health, nutrition, and fitness, and, more importantly, a whole point of view toward life. It involves the integration of the total individual—body, mind, and spirit, even our relationships with others—in achieving the best life possible.

To achieve high-level wellness, you need to understand basic ideas about nutrition, exercise, and health. Yet, once again, it is even more important to *know thyself*. You need to know who you are, who you want to be, and how health matters to you as a person. Wellness also matters for organizations, which is why the pursuit of high-level wellness by individuals makes sense as part of an enterprise solution for quality.

To thank is to express gratitude and acknowledgment. You can acknowledge your gratitude for your body every day with an awareness of nutrition, fitness, and the proper role of medicine. The following discussion of best practices has the feel of a patchwork quilt because the practices are coming from different sources and may not look alike. This reflects the fact that, unlike teamwork, where there is broad agreement on "what it looks like", there is not a consensus view of best practices in nutrition, fitness, and health to draw upon.

You may recall that in PerfectCoaches it is up to each person to decide. In this case, each person is deciding how to thank your body. In keeping with that spirit, the following discussion provides a representative list of best practices for nutrition, fitness, and health.

The first best practices can be thought of as the basic habits that determine what you put into your body and how you make sure it gets the exercise it needs. You also thank your body by the way you dress, manage your routine, and make decisions about the medications you introduce into it.

There are many approaches from which to choose. In the area of nutrition there is, for example, the view of T. Collin Campbell and Dr. Caldwell Esselstyn, presented in the movie *Forks Over Knives*, that animal-based foods along with processed foods are the source of many of our degenerative diseases. Fresh fruits and vegetables are the key to wellness, in this view.

The Atkins Diet, on the other hand, recommends limiting carbohydrates. In that view, consuming meat is encouraged because of its high protein content.

Adding to the confusion concerning best practices in nutrition, there are a number of what can be called "lifestyle" plans. The heart of many of these plans is a dramatic premise that has a great deal of appeal on the face of it. Often these plans include specific ideas for exercise and fitness. For example, there is Mark Sisson's "Primal Blueprint" presented in his book *21-Day Total Body Transformation*. Somewhat in accord with Loren Cordiant's *The Paleo Diet*, Sisson's concept is that humans are genetically designed for certain foods— and types of exercise regimens—and returning to them in the modern era is the key.

In the area of fitness, there are also several fault lines of disagreement concerning what constitutes best-practice. At some risk of oversimplification, the disagreements mostly involve the relative importance of cardiovascular exercise versus weight training. Generally, a cardiovascular exercise that improves breathing and circulation is a good starting point, with weight training used to sustain or improve muscle mass and tone.

There are even disagreements on the proper role of modern medicine. Part of the concern is a general over-reliance on prescription medicines of all sorts, particularly treatments for psychological issues.

Although sound medical practice does involve early diagnosis and treatment, many practitioners warn against using them excessively, reminiscent of the Hippocratic admonition to do no harm. An often-cited example of an overused procedure is routine screening for prostate cancer using the "PSA" (Prostate Specific Antigen) score.

Critics of the test point to long-term studies that call into doubt the number of lives saved and highlight the more easily documented emotional and physical complications of the procedures used, particularly prostate removal.

And finally, there are even competing views concerning how best to attain the inner experience often associated with high-level wellness. These range from an insistence on the need for relatively formal yoga or meditation practices to the idea that wellness is just an attitude that can be mastered in daily life, often by simple habits of thought.

In the midst of these sometimes-heated debates, there are many plans that could be called "middle-of-the-road", taking a common sense, how-to tone. Dr. Wayne Scott Andersen's *Discover Your Optimal Health* is an example.

It comes as no surprise that the suggested best practices for wellness, diet, and fitness are too numerous to mention. What is surprising is that they often contradict each other. Perhaps the single best comprehensive set of recommendations can be found in the *2015-2020 Dietary Guidelines for Americans*, a joint product of the U.S. Departments of Agriculture (USDA) and Health and Human Services (HHS).

The Dietary Guidelines note that "a large body of evidence now shows that healthy eating patterns and regular physical activity can help people achieve and maintain good health and reduce the risk of chronic disease throughout all stages of the lifespan." Although the guidelines are written for professionals, the following best practices, though stated broadly, are consistent with those guidelines and represent a common-sense approach similar to Andersen's *Discover Your Optimal Health*.

You can thank your brain by being mindful of its powers and giving it a small tap of acknowledgment every day. You can thank your body with more than a tap of acknowledgment. You can, and should, show your thanks by taking very good care of it.

Eating the right foods should be part of your daily routine. The same is true of exercise, whether it's walking, jogging, swimming, biking, weight training, yoga, or group exercise classes. The more you enjoy these things, the more likely you are to stick with them.

Set a Target

> *"No matter how you slice it, weight loss comes down*
> *to the simple formula of calories in, calories out."*
> *– Valerie Bertinelli*

Wellness is about nutrition, fitness, and the inner experiences of well-being. For many people, these converge in their body image, and more specifically, their weight. For most people, perhaps the single best way to tell if you are thanking your body is if you are maintaining a correct body weight. Hence to know, and strive for, a target body weight is an excellent starting point for all the wellness best practices.

People are less likely to mention their body image when answering the question, "Who am I?" than when discussing their future self. Body image is more of an external goal than a component of self for many people.

The first step is to determine a target body weight. You can select a numerical goal like "140 pounds." You can also do things to inspire and remind yourself, like getting an outfit for the body you want to strive for, then hanging it in your closet. There are many online calculators to do this. Usually, they quote a range based on height, age, and, in more sophisticated ones, bone structure. There are many web-based tools to help you set a target weight, including www.healthyeater.com/ideal-body-weight-calculator.

It is best to work with your primary care physician and to do so mindful of other important metrics like blood pressure. Although it poses challenges for many people, there is no need to regard hitting your target body weight as a mysterious process. Ultimately it is mostly about balancing caloric intake with caloric burn—eat better, eat less, move more.

It's a piece of cake, right? Pun intended. The key is to be mindful of your body weight goal and your real body weight. Although it can be counterproductive in some cases, one simple way to sustain focus on the goal is weigh yourself at least a couple of times each week.

Do Your To-Eat List

"Make every bite, every sip, a decision for pleasure,
a decision for health." – Anonymous

Eating the right things and exercising come together as part of a healthy daily routine.

Focus, first, on what you eat and drink. You are what you eat, the expression goes. Food and drink sustain our bodies and should also bring us pleasure. For most adults most of the time, what you eat is a conscious, affirmative choice. Begin each day with a "to-eat list", a fun and highly useful variation of a to-do list. It's a simple daily plan for what you will eat and drink, plus when and where you will have your meals and snacks.

To form this habit, start by making the simplest list possible based on what will help you reach or maintain your target weight. Find out how many calories are right for you. You can begin by working with 2,000 calories, sort of an average for everybody, or get an estimate geared to your body type from online tools such as www.calculator.net/calorie-calculator.html.

A fun thought experiment is to "think bananas." A banana is about 100 calories, so if you are a typical adult planning to eat 2,000 calories, that's equivalent to twenty bananas. Start with a calorie counter like www.nhs.uk/Tools/Pages/Calorie-checker.aspx.

Next, convert each of the foods on your to-eat list to an equivalent number of bananas (see Appendix 2 for examples), as if you were starting the day with a basket of bananas and exchanging them for, say, a McDonalds Fish Filet (379 calories, about 4 bananas). At the end of the day, see how closely you followed your list. If you exceed your banana count, you know you have made a decision to gain weight. If you have bananas left over, you've tried to lose weight. Your list will evolve over time as you learn what works.

A good to-eat list will have the right balance of carbs, protein, and fruits and vegetables adding up to roughly 2,000 calories. You will see immediately that having a to-eat list means knowing what you will *not* eat or drink that day. You can pick the foods on your list based on guidelines from the many health and nutrition plans discussed earlier, including www.who.int/nutrition/topics/5keys_healthydiet/en/.

Be sure your to-eat list includes plenty of water. As you refine your list, take into account the caloric content of drinks, both alcoholic and non-alcoholic. Also remember that when it comes to meals, super-sized isn't super. In the world of super-sized portions, dining out can be dangerous regardless of what you choose to eat.

There are habits that will help keep portion sizes small. Choose an appetizer instead of an entree, split a dish with a dining companion, or take some home to eat as another meal. To "test drive" this new habit, eat only half of the portion served the next time you eat out.

When you get into the habit of thanking your body with what you eat, you can thank specific parts of your body, as different aspects of nutrition have an impact on different organs, including the brain.

Omega-3 oils, found in walnuts, flaxseed, and especially fish, have long been touted as being healthy for the heart. But recent research suggests they're a brain booster as well, and not just because they help the circulation system that pumps oxygen to your head. They also seem to improve the function of the membranes that surround brain cells, which may be why some research indicates that individuals who consume a lot of fish are less likely to suffer depression, dementia, even attention-deficit disorder.

> ## Eat More Brain Foods
>
> These foods appear to enhance the performance of the nervous system and are dubbed "brain foods":
>
> - Walnuts
> - Olive oil
> - Bran
> - Coffee
> - Spinach
> - Dark chocolate
> - Avocados
> - Wheat germ
> - Beets
> - Water
>
> Each of these foods have their own distinct benefit.

PerfectCoaches suggests being thankful for a lot of things: our brain, our breath, our body, our life. Why not thank nature, too? Snacking is a good place to start good eating habits, and it is possible to *thank nature* when you snack. Just avoid processed snacks. There are many snack foods that are manufactured by humans using sugar and additives to make them delicious. As an alternative, when you snack, thank nature for the rainbow of fruits, vegetables, and nuts you can have instead. Nature provides a wide variety of delicious, healthy, and, yes, filling choices.

Deeply colored fruits and vegetables contain higher concentrations of vitamins, minerals, and antioxidants. Many vegetables including carrots, snow peas, and cherry tomatoes serve as excellent between-meal snacks. Nuts offer a variety of colors and tastes.

Your to-eat list isn't just about what you eat and drink, it involves where and when you do it. Some diets suggest eating six relatively light meals. Each person has their own style of eating, so find yours without being confined to a straight "three square meals" concept. It might help to pack fruit and other light snacks to keep your appetite manageable through the day.

Other plans suggest that you eat your last full meal of the day at a scheduled time, then literally fast until breakfast the next morning. It's hard to avoid eating at "after six" social occasions or when you are working in the evening. But, if possible, establish the habit of skipping heavy evening meals and snacks. Evening snacks are a difficult habit to break. Drinking lots of water after dinner can help make you feel full. Moving to very light snacks where you "thank nature" can also help.

Exercise 2% Plus

> *"If you breathe a little harder and stretch a little more,*
> *just simply moving can do wonders." – Anonymous*

Countless studies have demonstrated that exercise can improve how you feel and how you look. A useful guideline for exercise is that you should spend at least thirty minutes each day doing *something*. That's roughly 2% of a 24-hour day, which is why this foundational behavior is called "exercise 2% plus." The "plus" is an encouragement to do more when you can. You can plan when and where this exercise will happen with a simple sentence on the bottom of your to-eat list.

As you build a routine of low- to moderate-level exercise, or if you routinely exercise already, gradually increase the duration and intensity of your workouts. As noted earlier, there are many schools of thought concerning what fitness habits work best for a particular individual. Guidelines from the World Health Organization can form the basis of an exercise plan (see www.who.int/dietphysicalactivity/physical-activity-recommendations-18-64years.pdf).

Importantly, exercise is not just good for your body, it is good for your brain. Your brain is, first and foremost, a physical organ, and therefore can be nourished and exercised. Exercise improves the flow of blood in the brain just as it does in other organs. In addition, it can enhance the role of neurotransmitters involved in cognitive processes.

The simple best-practice for proper exercise is to get started and do *something*, do that something routinely, and enjoy doing it. Your routine should include a warm-up and cool down period, an awareness of the proper form for the exercises you are doing, and knowing your limits.

But, always, the goal is to do it, and enjoy it. Short-term diets and fitness programs can be helpful, but it is better to *change* your diet than *go on a diet*; it is better to *be fit* than to *get fit*. Lifestyle changes that become part of your normal routine are the key to lasting health.

Say Bravo to H₂0: Drink Plenty of Water

"I try to start drinking water as soon as my feet hit the
floor in the morning." – Mary Kay Andrews

Water deserves a round of applause. Water, by some estimates, constitutes 70 % of the human body. This includes brain tissue, and dehydration can cause your brain to shrink and pull away from the skull, triggering pain receptors surrounding the brain, resulting in a headache. Bottled water comes in many shapes, sizes, and brands because many people drink lots of water because they find it to be delicious.

In addition, drinking water helps flush waste products and toxins from your body, promotes healthy kidneys and bowels, increases skin elasticity, and boosts energy. Staying well hydrated will also help you make healthier food choices. Despite broad awareness of this, many people go through life dehydrated.

Although there is no one universally accepted "prescription" for how much water you should drink (six to eight glasses is a widely cited recommendation), strive to drink plenty of water and put an amount that feels right to you on your to-eat list.

Dress for Success

> *"Costly thy habit as thy purse can buy, But not expressed in fancy—rich, not gaudy, For the apparel oft proclaims the man." – William Shakespeare, Hamlet*

Good nutrition, exercise, and commitment to a target bodyweight demonstrate an appreciation of your body's importance. Another way you can thank your body is to dress it well. This involves not just the clothes you wear, but your grooming in general. Taken together, your skin, hair, and nails are the body's most visible organ, and everyone can see them every day.

Once again, there are many guidelines and concepts about how to dress and how to present yourself—and your body—to the world. In the 1970s, the books *Dress for Success* and *The Women's Dress for Success,* by John T. Molloy, described how what you wear can make a difference in your business and personal success.

Dressing for success can be complicated, or it can be simple. Every day, first thing in the morning when you look in the mirror before going out, and last thing in the evening, ask yourself: Did you thank your body by helping it look as good as it can look?

Make Health a Habit

> *"Healthy living is not a goal, it's a routine you build one habit at a time." – Anonymous*

Making health a habit means getting the finest medical and dental care you can afford, taking medicines and supplements as prescribed, and keeping the recommended schedule for preventive tests and examinations.

Like nutrition and fitness best practices, good health involves establishing a daily routine but, in addition, it involves setting monthly and yearly schedules.

By taking all prescribed medicines and brushing your teeth daily, you are making health a habit. Surprisingly, many people do not take the medications prescribed for them. In the Mayo Clinic proceedings of April 2011, it was reported that approximately 50% of patients do not take the medications they are prescribed. Whether or not this specific estimate is accurate, most medical practitioners understand that they cannot assume their patients have taken it at all or have taken it correctly.

A simple best-practice: take medicines as prescribed. Establishing this habit can be as easy as using a "pill organizer" labeled with the days of the week.

Because dentists recommend brushing your teeth at least twice daily, brushing your teeth is like taking a prescribed medication. This habit is so important that the American Dental Association has a website (part of Mouthhealthy.org) with video instructions. As with fitness activities, establishing a regular time and place with predictable cues and rewards generally makes sticking with habits like taking your meds and brushing your teeth easier.

Finally, to get the most from modern medicine, you should also keep a regular schedule of visits to your dentist and your family doctor or the person most familiar with your health needs. To make this more likely, post the dates and times of your next appointments in a place where you'll look at them frequently.

Just Ask *Why* to Drugs

"The best way to stop a bad habit is to never begin it."
– J.C. Penny

Drugs play a major role in medicine, but they have also become a leading cause of death. Being mindful of their effect is an important best-practice in modern life. "Just say 'no' to drugs" is a simple, useful catchphrase. It applied originally to harmful, addictive drugs taken by youth, but it can really apply to any drug taken by anybody, at any age, for any reason. But, when one considers all the drugs that are available and all the effects that they cause, perhaps a better way to look at it is to just ask *why* to drugs. A 2014 *Scientific American* article by Scott O. Lilienfeld and Hal Arkowitz traces the concept of saying "no" to drugs to 1982, when First Lady Nancy Reagan "uttered those three words in response to a schoolgirl who wanted to know what she should say if someone offered her drugs." It describes how "the first lady's suggestion soon became the clarion call for the adolescent drug prevention movement, in the 1980s and beyond." It seemed so simple: Just say "no."

Lilienfeld and Arkowitz argue that the programs have had disappointing results, although a review of the research literature did indicate "that the most effective ones involve substantial amounts of interaction between instructors and students."

"Rehearsing refusal" can be particularly useful "by asking students to play roles on both sides of a conversation about drugs, while instructors coach them about what to say and do."

The legal and medical definition of drugs and their effects is complex. In the United States at least, whether a drug is illegal or banned (for example, by the National Collegiate Athletic Association) does not necessarily tell you how bad it could be for you.

If you picture yourself as a physician prescribing medication for yourself, then ask why you ingest psychoactive substances, be they stimulants (ranging from everyday nicotine and caffeine to amphetamines, cocaine, and crack), depressants (cannabis, alcohol [or, more precisely, ethanol]), opioids (such as heroin, morphine, and codeine), or hallucinogens that results in unpredictable distortions of your perception of reality.

Addictive drugs can confuse your brain by flooding it with dopamine, the neurotransmitter that helps regulate movement, emotion, and feelings of pleasure. When activated at normal levels, dopamine rewards eating, sex, and other natural behaviors.

Overstimulation by drugs produces euphoria, reinforcing the addictive behavior of drug use. So, be sure to ask *why* when doing highly addictive drugs.

Being aware of how much we use drugs in our daily lives is useful. Caffeine is a drug. Having a cup of coffee is routine for most people. As a drug, caffeine has its place. Otherwise, we'd be left to wonder why God invented Starbucks. According to Mayoclinic.org, "up to 400 milligrams (mg) of caffeine a day appears to be safe for most healthy adults. That's roughly the amount of caffeine in four cups of brewed coffee, ten cans of cola or two 'energy shot' drinks."

Somewhere near that purveyor of caffeine there is likely to be a purveyor of wine, beer, and spirits. Quite possibly, they will be advertising a "happy hour." Although ingesting ethanol increases the depressive effects of the inhibitory neurotransmitter GABA, drinks in a social setting have their place.

Nicotine is a drug. Depending on where you are, it may be legal to have a smoke to go with that coffee or cappuccino. It also depends on where you are because smoking is banned in many public places. For more than half a century, since the 1964 U.S. Surgeon General's report, the health risks of tobacco have been known. So, before lighting up, ask *why*. Indeed, ask why to every drug. If there is no good reason, just say no.

Just asking why to any drug is a way to avoid addiction. This is especially important in the case of alcohol, opiates, or other drugs that make it difficult to function effectively. Those suffering from addiction must confront the issue with greater vigilance and fortitude because the stakes are high. Just as there are many factors contributing to addiction, there are many contributing factors that increase and decrease the chances of recovery.

One of the primary factors associated with recovery is accountability on the part of the person trying to recover. Accountability means being constantly mindful of the need to follow through on tasks or activities upon which their recovery depends.

In the next chapter, we will discuss additional building block behaviors to thank life. Because these final sets of best practices apply to life as a whole, it isn't necessarily useful to ask yourself every day if you did them. Rather, the question would be, are you mindful, perhaps every second of the day, of your commitment to live these best practices for life?

Change One Thing Now

John wants to lose weight but is continually frustrated by his attempts to diet. He decides to try a skillset for better results.

- He starts by setting a target weight, one that is reasonable and practical.
- He creates a weekly and daily to-eat list and use that for his shopping list.
- He adds in a brisk walk to and from the office, to get thirty minutes of exercise a day.
- He carries a liter water bottle to work, and keeps it filled so he can remember to drink more water.

As those building blocks of behavior stack up, he makes additional changes.

- He changes his attire to suits that make him feel more successful.
- He adds a gym membership and signs up for a spin class that he attends regularly.
- He doesn't rely on drugs and alcohol to relax; instead, he replaces those with healthy behaviors.

Chapter Seven
Live Well: Thank Your Life

You can thank your brain with an affectionate pat to the forehead. You keep reminding yourself how powerful it is, and you use it always.

You can thank your breath by paying close attention to it, even if just for a brief meditation session.

You can thank your body by eating what is good for it, giving it the exercise, it needs, and getting it the professional medical attention, it deserves.

But how do we thank life itself? Maybe the answer is as simple as "Just do it." The Roman Emperor and stoic philosopher Marcus Aurelius had this suggestion:

> *When you arise in the morning, think of what a precious privilege it is to be alive—to breathe, to think, to enjoy, to love.*

Thanking life also involves a particular facet of self-awareness, namely, understanding *what life means to you right now*. Viktor Frankl, to be discussed later, made this point:

> *The meaning of life differs from man to man, from day-to-day and hour to hour. What matters, therefore, is not the meaning of life in general but rather the specific meaning of a person's life at a given moment.*

Thank Life

What habits can make you more aware of what life means and why you should be thankful for it? There are many approaches, but three are suggested here.

Especially when life is presenting itself as the struggle that it truly is, it can be difficult to visualize a "to-be" you who is thankful to be part of that struggle. Sometimes professional help beyond the scope of PerfectCoaches is required. If you feel you need professional help, you should seek it immediately, perhaps calling 911 if the need for help seems urgent. In normal circumstances, however, you can be more thankful for your life if you build the right habits.

Thank Your Breath and Meditate

> *"One way to break up any kind of tension is good deep breathing." – Byron Nelson*

Engaging your *brain* and thanking it can bring success. Thanking your *breath* and being mindful of its powers can be just as important. The respiratory system, like the nervous system, is constantly at work, whether you are aware of it or not. They work together, in fact, to make life and mind possible. The breath, which brings in life-giving oxygen and expels carbon dioxide, is often equated with life itself. Breath is life.

Breathing takes place automatically under the control of a center at the base of the brain. The center sends signals to the breathing muscles of the lung to ensure that they contract and relax regularly. We don't have to think about it. But we can think about it, and when we do, we can control it to our advantage. You own your breath. It's a valuable possession and can be a valuable tool.

As David Disalvo discusses in *Forbes* online *(Breathing and Your Brain: Five Reasons to Grab the Controls),* you can do better physical and mental work when you have plenty of oxygen.

Breathing techniques are also important in the practice of *meditation*, a term that has many definitions in science, psychology, spirituality, and health practice. One can define meditation as, "To engage in mental exercise (as concentration on one's breathing or repetition of a mantra) for purposes of reaching a heightened level of spiritual awareness." As used in the PerfectCoaches context, the word spiritual does not require that meditation be about the creator, although prayerful meditation can always take place.

Mindfulness meditation, a variation of the practice that PerfectCoaches emphasizes, means experiencing the present moment more fully while meditating.

Just as there are many definitions of meditation, there is a whole range of options for using the technique. There are elaborate, formal rituals practiced by Buddhist monks and taught at day-long, week-long, even month-long retreats. At a simpler level, meditation can mean taking five minutes out of your day to be very still, close your eyes and breathe.

> **Controlled Breathing Exercise**: Inhale deeply through the nose for about five seconds, hold it, then take longer to exhale it through the mouth.

The goal almost always is to bring the mind and body together in a state of calmness and relaxation. Most techniques involve a quiet location, a comfortable posture (e.g., standing, sitting, lying down, or even walking), a focus of attention sometimes using specific words or mantras, and a mindful readiness to free yourself from distractions.

Whether you want to explore meditation techniques or simply get into the habit of thanking your breath, at a minimum, allow time to simply concentrate on your breathing. Do it the same time every day, at 9:00 am, for example.

The routine can be very simple. For example, begin with two or three very deep cleansing breaths, then begin to breathe normally. Be still and listen to your breath pass through your mouth and nose. Feel the movement of your lungs as you inhale and exhale. Let the time help you think clearly, feel calm, and be thankful.

Have you thanked your breathing and meditated today? Yes or No?

Change One Thing Now

To center herself and start the day off right, Jane concentrates on her breathing. She finds that doing so centers her and allows her to be more productive and calmer during the day.

How to Thank Your Breath: Close your eyes and try to clear your mind.

- Exhale through your mouth, a cleansing breath like a deep sigh.
- Inhale through your nose.
- Exhale through your mouth again.

Repeat this simple process for a minute or two, or longer if you can. Enjoy it. Master it. Use it when you're tense. Use it to meditate—relax and clear your mind—any time of day.

Be Your Own Friend

"If you're happy, if you're feeling good, then nothing else matters." – Robin Wright

A friend is *a person whom one knows and with whom one has a bond of mutual affection.* Learning to be your own friend is one single habit that opens the door to many specific best practices in life. It helps you know yourself better, like yourself more, and make the sound practical choices that a trusted friend would suggest. How do you acquire the habit?

First, to be your own friend means knowing yourself. The self-awareness snapshot in PerfectCoaches is designed to help make that happen. But to truly know yourself you have to allocate some time and attention, day-in and day-out, to watching yourself in action and understanding the meaning of what you do. The journal and virtual coach help you apply social intelligence, to be discussed shortly, to yourself.

Second, the inner experience of feeling a bond of affection *for yourself* can be deeply satisfying, in its own right. The PerfectCoaches process is designed to help you feel good about the person you are becoming. It feels good to have goals. It feels good to identify specific habits that will help you meet those goals. Perhaps most importantly, it feels good to be thankful for *you:* your brain, your body, your breath, and, of course, life itself.

A final way to be your own friend is to become a trusted advisor to yourself. For example, "friends don't let friends drink and drive." Would your best friend want you to drink and drive? Hopefully not. Then why should you let yourself do it?

You can give yourself more complicated advice: "Friends don't let friends go through life without having some sort of budget." Take that advice. You can follow the 50/30/20 rule for allocating 50% of your income to things you need (food, clothing, shelter, transportation, etc.), 30% to things you want, and 20% to savings. The 80/20 plan is even simpler: allocate 20% to savings and 80% to everything else. The challenge of saving 20% is at the heart of both plans (see www.thebalance.com/dont-like-tracking-expenses-try-the-80-20-budget-453602).

The PerfectCoaches journal and virtual coach help you be your own trusted advisor. Not every best-practice habit can be singled out in a book or an app, but many, like budgeting, fall under the heading of following your own good advice. Specific spending goals can be built into a to-do list, or you can identify a habit—e.g., stick to a budget—and master it.

Build a Life Team

> *"Alone we can do so little, together we*
> *can do so much." – Helen Keller*

Being your own friend is not a license for self-indulgence when you are part of a team of friends who care about each other. A group is a set of people interacting. A team is more than just a group. A team is special because it has shared goals and mutually understood roles. A successful sports team wins because each player knows his or her role. Success is defined as winning.

A successful life team consists of a network of win-win relationships that foster outcomes that benefit everybody. How do we assure that every relationship can function as a team that "wins" in the sense that it successfully meets its goals? One way is to be aware that the teams and teamwork discussed earlier are not just important at work, they are important in every aspect of life.

Many of the teams that are important to you are dyads, two-person teams consisting of you and one other person. Even in a two-person relationship, the doctrine of the four Ts is relevant. The more **Talking** ("this is what I think we should do"), **Training** ("please show me how you would like me to do this"), and **Thanking** that happens, the more likely it is that the **Team** will "win", i.e., reach the goals everyone is striving to achieve.

Having a good laugh with others is also a great team building exercise. The value of laughter is no joke. Most people would tell you that laughter helps them relax, feel better, and think better. The scientific explanation for this is that laughter release endorphins and other chemicals into our bloodstream.

We don't really need scientists to tell us that it feels good to laugh, and also to make others laugh along with us. Life is there for us to enjoy if we learn how to do it. A good laugh with friends can serve as a counterbalance to the stress and anxiety with which everyone has to deal. Some writers advocate a habit like "take ten minutes each day to have fun and laugh."

We share a good laugh when someone tells a joke or funny story. It also happens spontaneously when people see the humor in a situation. Either way, laughing can improve performance and health. Laughter is, to make what seems like an unavoidable pun, a serious matter.

There is even a science of laughter—*Gelotology,* from the Greek *gelos*, meaning laughter. It examines the causes of humor and laughter, as well as the physiological mechanisms associated with it.

Research shows that laughter relaxes muscles, releases pleasure-stimulating endorphins, stimulates breathing, and relieves stress. In some instances, it appears to improve clinical outcomes for cancer, and other diseases. Aside from this scientific evidence, it is difficult to disagree with the proposition that laughter is a good thing. Walt Disney said, "Laughter is America's most important export."

Your life team is more than a network of people. It is a safety net of sorts. Team building takes time and energy. As you deal with a person in different situations, you get better at interpreting their thoughts from their body language, facial expressions, and other non-verbal clues using the emotional intelligence to be discussed shortly. The more you know the people to whom you relate, and the more they know you, and the stronger the safety net of relationships becomes. The quote from Helen Keller is true: we do more together than alone. You are building, not just a life team, but a *winning* life team.

"Do Happy" Mindfully and Holistically

> *"Always be mindful of what feels good. Never return
> the gift of the moment you are in."* – Anonymous

It is true that life is downright sad at times. It is also true that some people suffer "major depression" or "clinical depression," a medical condition for which there are medical treatments. PerfectCoaches cannot change these facts.

On the other hand, for most people most of the time it is possible to "Do Happy," that is, it is possible to understand what makes us feel happy and do those things more often by living each day mindfully and holistically.

A case could be made for marking this best-practice with the sign for infinity (∞) in order to emphasize the breadth and depth of the idea. In mathematics, infinity is an abstract concept describing something without any limits, bigger than any number. In everyday language, infinity usually signifies something that goes beyond what we can count or understand.

This infinitely important habit of daily living brings three ingredients together. The first is that we can, to some extent, lead the emotional life we want to live by thinking of inner experiences, as behaviors that we can learn. This can be facilitated by the second ingredient: living each day mindfully, savoring the events taking place right now, in the present moment, in good times and bad. This has been discussed throughout the book. The third ingredient, living each day holistically, means seeing all aspects of your life as interconnected, best understood by experiencing each thing as part of a whole.

Holistic thinking is perhaps even more subtle than mindfulness. It means understanding the tangible benefits of good nutrition, regular exercise, and good health habits, but goes beyond them to an intangible sense of being in balance with the people and things that surround you.

Holistic living means emphasizing the integration of body, mind, spirit, and the habits of daily life. Living mindfully and holistically is to embrace life's patchwork of experiences as one continuous fabric. Mother Teresa, the Roman Catholic nun and humanitarian, described life this way:

> *Life is an opportunity, benefit from it;*
> *Life is beauty, admire it;*
> *Life is a dream, realize it;*
> *Life is a challenge, meet it;*
> *Life is a duty, complete it;*
> *Life is a game, play it;*
> *Life is a promise, fulfill it;*
> *Life is sorrow, overcome it;*
> *Life is a song, sing it;*
> *Life is a struggle, accept it;*
> *Life is a tragedy, confront it;*
> *Life is an adventure, dare it;*
> *Life is luck, make it;*
> *Life is too precious, do not destroy it; and*
> *Life is life, fight for it.*

Being thankful for life invites questions about the source of life. Should someone or something be thanked? Religions vary widely in their deities, rituals, and creation stories. Anthropological studies (see for example Peoples, etal., Human Nature, 2016) show that animism, the belief that a supernatural power dwells in all things, is present in every primitive society and may be the first form of religion to emerge. In the book Why God Won't Go Away, neuroscientist Andrew Newberg makes the still controversial case that a need for God and spirituality is hardwired into the human brain. Whether that is true or not, each faith enables its believers to understand where their lives fit within the universe and all of creation. For some people, a creator-spirit or revered deity becomes part of their life team, perhaps the central figure in it.

There can be a spiritual dimension to holistic self-awareness. It embraces creation as an extension of the self, and the self as a part of creation. Some belief systems equate God with nature, and nearly every belief system, even atheism, acknowledges that we experience life within a creation greater than ourselves. Believing that the self and creation are in balance, or *can* be, provides a certain inner peace, a state of psychological or spiritual calm.

The PerfectCoaches method is neutral about which psychological theories are valid or which religious beliefs contain the truth. It can work alongside of any theory or belief system, or by itself, as a source of insight into the connections between mind, wellness, spirit, and life. It is particularly compatible with religious faiths that believe the creator dwells within human beings and is revealed directly to each person.

Holistic living means understanding that self-awareness and behavioral focus not only apply to specific behaviors but also to the total self, which is something more. The self consists of the roles you play, the things you do that you and others can see—this has been our focus thus far—and inner experiences known only to you.

Inner experiences may, in fact, be the key to thanking life. They are also *behaviors*—thoughts or emotions we *do* in the process of adjusting to our environment.

Instead of saying "I am happy" or "I am sad" or "I am angry," you could say "I am doing happy," "I am doing sad," "I am doing angry," and so forth, even if we are doing them while doing other things that are visible to the world. We are what we repeatedly do, and it is possible to make "Do Happy" a behavioral goal by understanding what triggers and reinforcers create the inner experience of happiness. One way to learn the habit is simple. Do at least one thing each day just for the purpose of experiencing the positive feeling you get. Do something that you would not do otherwise, just to feel good. Although "doing happy" can have benefits like increased levels of serotonin and dopamine (a hormone and neurotransmitter associate with positive feelings) in your body, the test is whether doing that thing gives you the inner experience of feeling happy.

A 24x7 camera watching everything you do would observe your skills and habits but would not have access to what you feel inside. What if it focused only on your face? Your facial expressions can reflect your inner experiences. For example, you might spend half your time smiling, indicating satisfaction with your work or your environment or yourself.

Researcher Paul Ekman proposed a basic list of emotions shown in the expression on a person's face. He argued that these expressions are common to all humans and, importantly, mean the same thing across cultures. There are many variations of the list, but a relatively broad agreement that these emotions are accompanied by recognizable facial expressions:

- Anger
- Disgust
- Fear
- Contempt
- Happiness
- Sadness
- Surprise

These emotions are often referred to as the "basic emotions" all humans recognize in other people and as internal experience. The scientific work in this area is still evolving, and the list of common emotions may be much longer. The important point is that emotions are experienced by all humans, and they are revealed by facial expressions.

This list of facial expressions and emotions provides a starting point for understanding your inner experiences. You often use the words in Ekman's list—*I am angry, I am afraid, I am happy, I am sad*, etc. Inner experiences can be as simple as these one-word emotions, or much more complex combinations of inner thoughts and feelings, that can be difficult, perhaps impossible, to express in words.

In PerfectCoaches, the goal is to understand that inner experiences are a part of our core selves. Each person is aware, to some degree or another, that what they feel and think matters. Some approaches to self-awareness, in fact, encourage "getting in touch" with a mostly hidden "inner child" that carries childlike traits (e.g., joy, curiosity, and spontaneity) and childhood emotional experiences (e.g., fear and anger) into adulthood.

Inner experiences have two components. First, there are thoughts we keep to ourselves. Second, there are feelings, i.e., emotions. While we might be able to articulate our thoughts in words, the task is more difficult for emotions. To understand why, it is useful to review the basic science of the brain.

The brain has several regions. Two are important for this discussion. The *amygdala,* deep inside the skull, is the region generally responsible for emotions and emotional reactions.

Emotions are events in which one region of the brain, the amygdala, responds to the environment by releasing chemicals into the body. These include adrenaline and cortisol, the so-called stress hormones involved in "fight, flight, or freeze" reactions, and the "pleasure" hormones dopamine, oxytocin, serotonin, and endorphins. We can think of these as the "emotional brain."

The *frontal cortex* is the seat of intelligence, concept formation, problem-solving, and other "higher" mental processes. Located right at your forehead where you tapped your brain to thank it, it is the "thinking brain."

In some instances, the amygdala can respond to events in the environment before the "thinking brain" has fully processed them. It can be the case that the frontal cortex labels an emotion, often imprecisely, after it is already taking place and in effect "guesses" what caused the emotion and what conceptual label should be applied to the feeling.

This is a simplified view of the process, but for any inner experience, a useful first step is to "name it"—i.e., find words for the feeling or thought.

Once you have words for the experience, you can decide if you want to "tame it", i.e., control the feeling to the extent possible, or "proclaim it", i.e., acknowledge that the experience is an integral part of who you are, then build upon that fact. We do this naming, taming, and proclaiming for ourselves, but also for the benefit of the people around us.

Trying to express our inner experiences in spoken words invites another person to join your inner dialog with the Coaches. In his book, *Mindsight: The New Science of Personal Transformation*, Daniel Siegel presents a framework for interacting with other people that can eventually shed light on "the internal workings of our minds."

A key concept in Siegel's work is that an individual develops and grows within a matrix of human relationships, what PerfectCoaches calls a *life team*. This is true in infancy, childhood, and adulthood. Living mindfully and holistically invites you to understand not just your inner experiences, but also the inner experiences of the people with whom you interact. It can help you build the skills described as social intelligence or *emotional intelligence.*

Emotional intelligence, referred to as EI or EQ, can be an important tool. There is a substantial body of research on how emotional intelligence is acquired and how it works in social settings. The concept has some controversy associated with it, especially the claims that EQ can be more important than IQ (measured intelligence) for success.

The more aware we are of our own experiences, the easier it is to understand the experiences of others. In other words, as a person sharpens their skill at knowing who they are and what they do, particularly their inner experiences, there is a natural tendency to apply that understanding to others. Most definitions of emotional intelligence include the following elements:

- An awareness of your own emotions or inner experiences;
- The ability to give a name or label to your inner experiences;
- The ability to use emotional information to guide your own behavior;
- The ability to recognize the emotions and inner experiences of others; and
- The ability to use emotional information to understand and influence the behavior of others.

Daniel Goleman's book *Emotional Intelligence: Why It Can Matter More Than IQ* is an interesting discussion of emotional intelligence. It includes the concept of an "Amygdala Hijack", the situation where, in effect, emotional reactions take over before the person has time to think about what they are doing. It's useful to know that science is studying the events taking place within the nervous system, but you can't see them. All you see is behavior.

In PerfectCoaches, self-awareness, mindfulness, and emotional intelligence intersect. The method allows you to develop each one separately, and then use them together. Each concept is a bit different but using them in combination enriches our lives and helps us to be effective with others.

With this discussion of the total self—our roles, behavior, and inner experiences—we come full circle. It's all about who you are, where you want to go, and, as shall be discussed next, how you use feedback to get there.

Change One Thing Now

Jane has faced several challenges in the last year with a sick family member and end of a relationship that created some depression. She decided to change her thinking and instead of bemoaning her circumstances, she opted to thank life. She created this behavioral change by:

- Reading books and making a list of goals that were achievable and realistic
- Expanding her network to include more supportive friends
- Beginning and ending each day with a short meditation

Part Three

Feedback

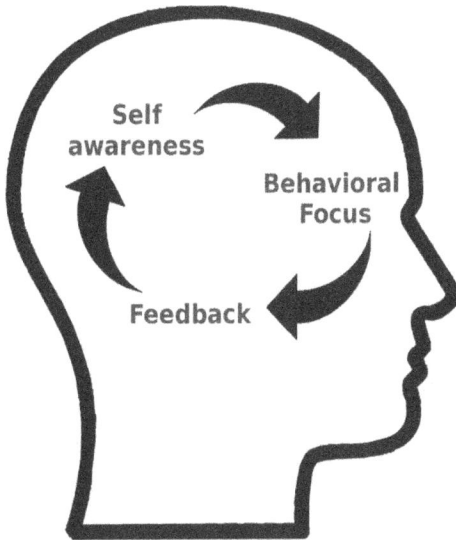

Self awareness

Behavioral Focus

Feedback

Chapter Eight
Your Journal, Your Connections

A journal is a personal record of events and how the writer reacts to them. Two very different journals—*The Diary of a Young Girl* by Anne Frank and *The Journals of Lewis and Clark* by William Clark and Meriwether Lewis—are among the best known, even though the writers are famous largely because of their journals. The journals of people like Winston Churchill, Thomas Jefferson, and Helen Keller, famous in their own right, also make fascinating reading.

In PerfectCoaches the journal doesn't only record events, it guides and shapes them. To continue to evaluate and make changes, a journal is an invaluable tool. If you pause each day to take a "me minute" and think about what you are doing *for you*, you can focus on changes you are trying to make to your habits, skills, and other behaviors. Making a journal entry every day, preferably at the same time of day, is the first habit you learn with PerfectCoaches. It helps you stay mindful of the behavior you are trying to learn, and you deserve spending a minute or two each day to think about the progress you are making and, just important, connecting with your virtual coach.

At this point in the process, you are aware of who you are and who you want to be. You have reviewed a menu of best practices. You can focus on any of these, or you can decide on some other behavior you would like to start or stop. The next challenge is to convert that behavioral focus to results, and your PerfectCoaches journal is a resource toward that end.

There are three ways to keep a PerfectCoaches journal. One is simply to write observations on paper, allowing that process to reinforce your mindfulness of what you do. The Pen and Paper Workbook provides for thirty days of short entries. The thirty-day period reflects the observation that the practice of making journal entries every day, or most days, can help people master three new habits in thirty days. This is sometimes called the "3-in-30 goal."

The second way is to maintain your journal online and have someone read your journal entries and respond with questions, in the spirit of the Socratic dialog. This person may also be providing you with traditional coaching and mentoring.

The third way is to make journal entries online and interact with the virtual coach provided as part of the PerfectCoaches app. The coach's role is to provide feedback that motivates you to make short journal entries. Journaling once a day can help you stay mindful of your behavioral change goal throughout the day. This, in turn, gets you to "Got It!"—the self-assessed mastery of a new habit or skill.

Feedback is an interesting concept. As used in everyday speech, it refers, generally, to an evaluation of performance:

"I got some very positive feedback about that paper I wrote."

"The feedback from my coach boiled down to having to try a lot harder." "I'm still waiting for feedback on how you thought dinner went last night."

As a technical term in cybernetics, biology, and other disciplines, it can have a more neutral meaning denoting the effect of some action being "fed-back" to the system so as to influence the next thing the system does.

In PerfectCoaches, the coach provides feedback to a journal entry in the form of a brief question. This feedback reinforces the behavior of journaling; in other words, it improves the probability that you will make another journal entry. The purpose is not to evaluate or give guidance, but simply to provide feedback in the form of "food for thought" and sustain the behavior of making journal entries. This, in turn, sustains and reinforces behavioral focus.

The feedback provided by PerfectCoaches goes beyond the focused Socratic dialog around changing one specific habit. You receive feedback concerning your capacity to master your own behavior. Changing three behaviors in thirty days, for example, can be a beginning level of mastery. It is also possible to master, say, all the best practices discussed in this book, or others you may choose.

The journal supports the PerfectCoaches thought experiment. Thought experiments, as defined in *The Stanford Encyclopedia of*

Philosophy, are "devices of the imagination used to investigate the nature of things. They are used for diverse reasons in a variety of areas, including economics, history, mathematics, philosophy, and the sciences, especially physics." Albert Einstein imagined himself riding a light beam in one of his most famous thought experiments. Einstein's goal was to use concrete examples to help better understand abstract ideas.

The PerfectCoaches thought experiment rests on the Socratic dialog. When Socrates said, "The unexamined life is not worth living," he was not just defending his own philosophy. He was encouraging others to rely upon the simple truth that posing the right questions is the foundation of understanding.

The Socrates described in literature, a bearded old man in a swirling toga, is nothing like the coaches of today, directing and encouraging their players. He would hold forth in the Agora, an open marketplace near the Acropolis in ancient Athens, not seeming to direct much of anything. It was almost like he was chatting people up on a street corner or in a shopping mall.

Yet the common and prominent people who came to the Agora to do business often fell into a dialog with him. The other person would arrive at their own answers because of the questions Socrates asked. In other words, his questions did the coaching.

Imagine that Socrates traveled to the information age and had a chance to be a virtual coach. Unlike the complex questions he asked in the dialogs recorded by his student Plato, he could just ask short questions to provide food for thought and keep people moving forward.

Although you could imagine Socrates himself as your coach, PerfectCoaches lets you choose the person to engage with you in the Socratic dialog. No matter who that coach is, keeping a journal brings the thought experiment alive for your enjoyment and growth.

Your Virtual Coach

PerfectCoaches uses the word "coach" in very specific ways. First, the perfect coaches are not people, but rather fundamental questions of life. The coaching comes from the internal dialog of continuously asking, and answering, those questions. The coach enhances this process. From the time the coach begins asking questions in the

PerfectCoaches app, the interaction is not unlike motivational interviewing, first discussed by William R. Miller and Stephen Rollnick as a therapeutic tool but later applied to many types of personal development. The goal is to motivate you, help you understand that you are responsible for your own behavior, and foster "change talk" about specific changes in what you actually do in daily life.

Second, the role of the virtual coach does not involve traditional coaching activities like showing you how to do things, meeting in person to discuss specific issues and brainstorming what to do or providing examples of how other clients tackled various issues. Rather, the behaviors and skills you are learning are usually defined in advance, and the coach responds to journal entries where you assess your progress toward mastering the behavior. The coach asks questions that motivate you to continue your journal.

Journaling, in turn, sustains and reinforces the mindfulness and behavioral focus that get you from setting change goals to "Got It!" Consistent with the PerfectCoaches emphasis on simplicity, the journaling process itself can take less than a minute and a few words.

If you think you did very well, use words like: *absolutely, tops, great, terrific, on-target, best,* or phrases like, *got it right.* If you think you did okay, use words like *tried, except, maybe, next time.* If you didn't do well at all, tell your journal. Use words like: *abysmal, awful, frustrated,* and *upset.*

Your virtual coach will see your journal entry. PerfectCoaches can provide a coach, or you may select one. This is a modern version of the Socratic Method with the important exception that the dialog is about one thing only: what you *do.* Your journal entries should be short, and the coach will only ask a short question, which might be a question that has already been asked.

Your job is to not to respond to the comment, but rather to think it over as you become more aware of the cues and triggers that prompt your behavior. This internal reflection is the foundation of the PerfectCoaches thought experiment.

When you have mastered a new habit or skill, say, "Got It!" Your coach will know you can move to the next challenge. Sometimes you will see something that could be changed other than you. As part of the 24x7 virtual continuous improvement (Kaizen) process for your enterprise, just say "What if" at the beginning of your journal entry. Self-awareness, behavioral focus, and feedback let you perfect an approach to learning new habits that work best for you.

The person asking the questions could be anybody. It could be an influential mentor in your life. It could be a fictional character you find interesting, let's say one of the eccentrics from *The Big Bang Theory* series. It could be one of the characters out of Charles Sheldon's novel *In His Steps* where people wonder "What Would Jesus Do?"—although, in this case, it would be, "What question would Jesus ask?"

Importantly, even if a coach is a person you know, the PerfectCoaches thought experiment lets you imagine them as, doing their job flawlessly by being:

- Perfectly patient;
- Perfectly focused on the future;
- Perfectly committed to simplicity;
- Perfectly focused on results; and
- Perfectly at ease with the human condition.

Regardless of whom you select, you should be able to imagine the sound of their voice and see them in your mind's eye. Be creative in making this happen. Use your imagination. The goal is to foster an inner dialogue.

Full Socratic dialogs, a genre developed in Greece before the Christian Era, often involve elaborate arguments and, just as often, elaborate phrases and grammar appropriate to the ancient Greek culture. Full, elaborate dialogs are not well suited to the modern online world of short text messages and tweets. Nor are they well suited to the simplicity of PerfectCoaches.

Yet PerfectCoaches does preserve the crucial element of discovery via a dialog of questions and answers. Insight comes in Socratic fashion via questions. It is said that the mother of Socrates was a midwife and that he claimed to bring out wisdom that was already inside a person, much like a midwife helps give birth to a baby.

Two Ways to Use the Journal Questions

Gaining Insight

Think of The Coaches as people who would bring insight out of you by asking the following kinds of questions:

- Who can serve as a model for this behavior?
- Have you solved problems like this before?
- Is someone working against you, or are you working against yourself?
- Would your inner accountant want you to stop this behavior?
- What would your inner craftsman do to improve this?
- What is one thing you could do tomorrow to fix this?
- What happened immediately before you did this?
- What happened immediately after you did this?
- Is this making you feel worse, better, or neither?
- What will you do different the next time?
- What habits do you have that are getting in the way?

Understanding Consequences

Sometimes the questions can be focused on the antecedents and consequences of behavior, as discussed in connection with how you change. Examples would include:

- What event acts as a cue for that behavior?
- What positive or negative consequences follow that behavior?
- Who can encourage the substitution of a new behavior and provide positive reinforcement?
- What habits do you have that are getting in the way?

The PerfectCoaches virtual coach has the special role of reading your journals online and providing feedback following a ground rule for a Socratic dialogue: every response will be a question, one that you can answer for yourself to keep the virtuous cycle moving forward.

Everyone has had managers, mentors, colleagues, and friends who have provided feedback and encouragement during their life. Some of these people were more patient or more accepting than others. You can think of the virtual coach as meeting the criteria of a perfect coach, even though, if you select a real person for the role, they will not, of course, be perfect.

In PerfectCoaches, the motivational coach role consists primarily of providing feedback to the journal. Therefore, the coach can be a person you don't know but has expertise in providing feedback. Instead of that, or in addition to it, you may want to select a real living person who can have a dialogue with you about the reasons you do, and don't, change your behavior. This real person doesn't have to be perfect. They simply help you sort out the details of your personal and/or professional life and the specific activities you want to add, stop, or change as you improve your "As-Is" self and become your "To-Be" self.

PerfectCoaches presumes that changes in the roles you play and the behaviors you exhibit often, but not always, change your inner experiences. Ultimately, you are simply changing what you do.

Since, you are what you repeatedly do, you change by doing different things and doing the same things differently.

No matter how you plan to change, the virtual coach keeps the focus on specific behaviors and habits. In *Principles of Psychology* (1890) William James, one of the founders of psychology, famously said that habit is *the enormous fly-wheel of society*. When you rise each morning, you are in some respects already programmed to go through the day doing things the way you did them yesterday.

Importantly, James emphasized that habits either move us forward or hold us back in a quotation that reflected the views of his time. We have a portion of this quote earlier in the book, but it is worth exploring in more depth here:

> *Habit is thus the enormous fly-wheel of society, its most precious conservative agent...*
>
> *It dooms us all to fight out the battle of life upon the lines of our nurture or our early choice, and to make the best of a pursuit that disagrees...*
>
> *Already at the age of twenty-five you see the professional mannerism settling down on the young commercial traveler, on the young doctor, on the young minister, on the young counselor-at-law. You see the little lines of cleavage running through the character, the tricks of thought, the prejudices, the ways of the 'shop,' in a word, from which the man can by-and-by no more escape than his coat-sleeve can suddenly fall into a new set of folds.*
>
> *The great thing, then, in all education, is to make our nervous system our ally instead of our enemy. It is to fund and capitalize our acquisitions and live at ease upon the interest of the fund. For this we must make automatic and habitual, as early as possible, as many useful actions as we can, and guard against the growing into ways that are likely to be disadvantageous to us...*

The emphasis on making useful actions automatic and habitual is so important that we have revisited this quote here. This should be done as early in your life as possible, but it is never too late to change old habits and form new ones.

Science has discovered a great deal about habit-formation since 1890 when William James published *The Principles of Psychology*. For example, in his recent book, *The Power of Habit: Why We Do What We Do in Life and Business,* Charles Duhigg provides a modern, non-technical description of how cues in the environment stimulate behavior which is then reinforced in one way or another.

On his webpage, Duhigg tells the story of an Army Major who seemed to understand that riots in Iraq were caused by habits that could be changed simply by changing how food carts were arrayed. "The U.S. military," the major told Duhigg, "was one of the biggest habit-formation experiments in history. Understanding habits is the most important thing I've learned in the army," he said. "It's changed everything about how I see the world. You want to fall asleep fast and wake up feeling good? Pay attention to your nighttime patterns and what you automatically do when you wake up. You want to make running easy? Create triggers to make it a routine."

PerfectCoaches suggests that you focus on one behavior at a time. This is consistent with what the real estate entrepreneur and author Gary Keller, advocates when he talks about "The One Thing" you can do that can make other things you do easier and more effective. In PerfectCoaches, you would decide how to begin doing that one thing, or, if you already do it, spend more time and do it better.

Each person uses PerfectCoaches differently. Although the idea of self-awareness seems simple enough, the method is like a Rorschach test, the psychological technique where people describe what they think they see while viewing formless, ambiguous inkblots. What people describe when they look at the inkblot—or, in this case, the PerfectCoaches method—is what their mind prepares them to see.

Some people see the title *Life's 7 PerfectCoaches* and expect a book about self-improvement, like Steven Covey's *7 Habits of Effective People*. Interestingly, both books have the number seven in the title. Although there is nothing special about the number, there is a thing called Miller's Magic Number 7, Plus or Minus 2. It's a theory that human short-term memory works with between five and nine things, such as seven-digit phone numbers.

Most organizations and many people will say their goal is "to improve" one thing or another—efficiency, the quality of their work, their life as a whole. These individuals and organizations are attracted to the words *Perfect* and *Coach* in the title. They often consider themselves effective already, and they just want to be more methodical about "getting to the next level."

As a self-development method, whether practiced individually, in teams, or throughout an organization, PerfectCoaches clarifies goals and focuses on one behavior at a time. People experienced in self-development techniques are often inclined to go back and give a lot of thought to questions like "*Why* Do I Do It?" and "*When* Do I Do It Best?" They will enjoy having journals that record how they are creating their future self and building a better world.

Others look beyond the virtuous cycle of self-awareness, behavioral focus, and feedback to see PerfectCoaches as a complete philosophy for organizational and individual development. Although it's not *about* the academic subject of philosophy, PerfectCoaches, particularly the advanced thought experiments, does encourage the love and pursuit of wisdom, which is the definition of philosophy.

Many readers welcome the notion that life's great questions could be posed in the Socratic style to the whole of the modern world. The Socratic method offers a complete approach to fact-finding and critical thinking. It is one of the great intellectual achievements of civilization. Like the scientific method, it requires us to either clarify assumptions or eliminate them altogether through the relentless pursuit of facts.

Your Teams

PerfectCoaches harnesses the power of people, process, and technology. It is nearly impossible to place enough emphasis on the role that people around us play in serving as models for best-practice behaviors and sources of reinforcement for both effective and ineffective behavior.

New behaviors, habits, and skills are acquired in real life, day-to-day situations, often when you are working as part of a team. This is also where old habits are reinforced. Especially in the workplace, this means that members of work teams are providing positive and negative reinforcement to each other.

As noted earlier a team can be as small as two people, a dyad, working for a common goal. Sports teams can have twenty or thirty people, and an entire organization with thousands of employees in a hundred countries can refer to itself as a team. Going all the way back to Freud's analysis of an infant and its mother, the primordial human team, it can be said that people *happen* in teams, indeed, that all of society *happens* in teams.

That brings us to the doctrine of the four Ts, which we have mentioned a couple times before in this book. The workforce for a small business might be one or two teams, organized by shifts perhaps. In large organizations, the workforce might be organized by geography or by specialized function. Whichever applies, the best organizations get high-quality performance from the workforce by working with them as Teams. That is the first "T" in his doctrine.

The other three Ts — *Talk, Train, Thank,* — suggest the following ways to help teams be successful:

- Leaders and team members should *talk* about goals, communicating expectations as clearly as possible.
- Members of a team should *train* to acquire the necessary skills and habits.
- *Thanking* individuals for a job well done is crucial.

Basically, the doctrine of four Ts says people succeed in teams, and teams succeed because of the talking, training, and thanking that occurs within the team. PerfectCoaches facilitates all these processes. For example, a list of best-practice behaviors adopted by an organization "talks", i.e., communicates, to teams and individuals about the expectations of the organization. The entire process of journaling and feedback facilitates training and thanking.

Since PerfectCoaches is an enterprise solution, the role of teams is an important part of the planning. Even though people make decisions and do their work as individuals, they are part of teams who influence each other, reinforce each other's behavior, even train, and teach each other. If you look, you'll see examples everywhere.

Team

The first T in the doctrine says you should always think of those around you as team performers. We are social creatures. We get things done in groups. Each of us is an individual with our own track record, but success depends on being able to get the most out of the teams you interact with, either at work or in your personal life. Not only are those you interact with a source of feedback regarding your own behavior, but it is also possible to decide upon common goals for behavioral alignment and pursue those goals using PerfectCoaches.

Thinking of colleagues as part of your team helps at every level in an enterprise. At the very top of an organization, leaders work in teams composed of confidantes and trusted advisors. Visualize the head of your organization or, say, a large multi-national organization. They may have enormous individual talent and responsibility, but they fail or succeed because of the teams they belong to and lead. Rank-

and-file employees are aligned in teams that interact every day, either in person, or virtually, or both.

Talk

If you are a leader or manager, either formally or informally, the second T, talk to them, emphasizes the important role proactive communication about plans and goals can play. This is an important idea in mindful leadership, but it also applies to individuals who are simply working with each other. It helps to tell people around you what is going to happen and why.

Train

The third T refers to training. Many organizational change and quality improvement initiatives that try to build a culture of quality emphasize cultural values and the attitudes that go with them. Yet changing your attitudes is not enough. You must change specific behavior, which almost always requires formal training, as discussed earlier in the book. Our own experience tells us that getting reliable performance from people requires that they understand what to do, practice doing it, and get reinforcement for doing it right. There are many excuses and practical barriers that short-shrift training. Training is crucial, and PerfectCoaches can reinforce the new behaviors that are learned.

Thank

The fourth T in the doctrine is to thank. This final element of the Doctrine of Four Ts emphasizes the fact that people respond to rewards and incentives, both monetary and non-monetary. Once again, thanking people is not just for leaders; it is for everyone. Organizations build monetary incentives and bonuses into the process, when possible, but it is often more important to encourage praise and recognition within the team and throughout the larger workforce.

Saying "thank you" is not just polite, it is helpful to all concerned. When you thank another person, who has done something for you, all other things being equal, it will make it more likely that they will do it again. In a similar way, when they thank you, it reinforces the actions for which they are thanking you.

In the PerfectCoaches method, the talking, training, and thanking that goes on in teams is not a top-down process controlled by leaders and managers. Rather, it is just as important that the processes take place "laterally", i.e., for teammates to talk, train, and thank each other.

The PerfectCoaches app makes it possible for peers to coach each other by viewing and commenting on journal entries. Reports enable individuals to compare their progress with that of other members of their team, and teams to compare their progress with other teams and the organization as a whole.

Change One Thing Now

At the end of every day, Jane writes in her journal and takes note of the roadblocks in her quest to be punctual. She lists the goals she met, and the goals she is still working toward. At the end of the month, using all the PerfectCoaches tools, she has conquered her punctuality issues and is at work and in meetings on time.

What about for you? Using a journal can make a huge difference in your results. Although no one is perfect, keeping track of your own skills with PerfectCoaches, gives you the opportunity to strive to perform target behaviors 100% of the time.

Choosing two behaviors, for example, can become a focus as you work on those skills:

When working in your journal, note whether you were mindful of being punctual for all classes, meetings and events and completing assignments on schedule? Were you punctual every time? Yes, or No?

Were you mindful of the need to listen? When others spoke, did you look at them and let them finish their thought? Did you go through your day listening attentively without interrupting others? Yes, or No?

Chapter Nine
A Thought Experiment in Leadership

The basic PerfectCoaches thought experiment asks you to imagine an inner dialog with coaches who personify questions. An inner accountant asks why you spend time doing things, an inner craftsman asks when do you do your best work, and an inner planner asks where you are taking your life and career. The virtual coach can facilitate that inner dialog.

But that is only the beginning. Your own imagination sets the limits for the PerfectCoaches thought experiment. It invites you to imagine people you have known, famous people, even fictional characters serving as a source of feedback, motivation, and ideas. You can adopt those people as a standard to meet and imagine a dialog with them in which they provide feedback to you as you hone key skills and habits.

One possibility is to pick this coach based on things they have said either to you directly, in real life, or in some quotation. If you do an internet search looking for quotes from people who have actually been coaches, they are available on a variety of sites. Examples include:

> *A good coach will make his players see what they can be rather than what they are.* – Ara Parasheghian, football coach at Notre Dame

> *If you can't accept losing, you can't win,* and *It's not whether you get knocked down, it's whether or not you get up.* — Vince Lombardi, professional football coach

Sometimes you learn more from losing than winning.
Losing forces you to reexamine. – Pat Summit,
basketball coach at the University of Tennessee

Change One Thing Now

Conduct your own advanced thought experiment with a "celebrity motivation coach." It can be fun, interesting, and rewarding.

First, pick a figure known for his or her greatness, like the leaders discussed here, or pick a person you find interesting, even if they are not famous. It can be a celebrity or someone you've personally known.

Now imagine that the celebrity motivation coach read your journal entries and asked a question to provide you with feedback. Did his or her question help you understand why you did well or why you did poorly? Mull over the comment until you make your next journal entry.

Continuing this dialog in your journal can help you step outside yourself to analyze your behaviors and make corrections.

Historical figures and celebrities can also serve as your virtual coach. There are many lists of candidates from which to choose. *Biography Online* offers a *List of Top 100 Famous People* that includes actors, artists, politicians, entrepreneurs, sportsmen, and religious figures. *Forbes* Magazine's *Celebrity 100* lists the 100 highest-paid celebrities. A thought experiment imagining feedback from these famous figures can definitely stretch your imagination.

The Leadership Skillset

Advanced thought experiments can take any form. Because most people know about current leaders and famous leaders from history, and because leadership is so important, the skillset for leadership is presented here in the context of a thought experiment. What if you could engage in a dialog with one or more of history's great leaders?

Who are history's great leaders? One list is offered by Patrick Alain in *Industry Leaders* magazine. He suggested **Mahatma Gandhi, George Washington, Abraham Lincoln, Adolf Hitler, Muhammad, Mao Zedong, Nelson Mandela, Julius Caesar, Fidel Castro, and Winston Churchill.** Because Alain's list is thought-provoking—for instance, it can be argued that Hitler and **Mao Zedong relied more on coercion than persuasion**—it is quoted at length, highlighting the leaders particularly astute at face-to-face persuasion: Mahatma Gandhi, Abraham Lincoln, Nelson Mandela, and Winston Churchill.

Leadership has been defined as a process through which a person influences and motivates others to get involved in the accomplishment of a particular task. This single definition, although universally accepted, fails to define the paths and ways of people who are deemed great leaders. All great leaders had something unique about them and yet they were bound by the greatness that helped them to lead masses, to innovation and new ideologies.

Since the oldest known times, masses have been led by efficient leaders. Such men and women have been responsible for ushering their people into a new and more modern world as we know of it now. Although times have changed, the contributions of these great leaders cannot be forgotten and although practices and ways of doing things have changed as well, the ways of these great leaders cannot be overlooked. What made them great might still be applicable in today's day and age. Here is a look at some of the greatest leaders of all time and what made them great:

Mohandas Karamchand Gandhi, better known as Mahatma Gandhi, was born an ordinary boy with a determination to excel at what he did. After completing law school in London, he became the most important figure in the Indian struggle for freedom against colonial rule. His policy of non-violence and protest through civil disobedience eventually succeeded when he led his country to freedom in 1947. His main characteristics were **resilience, knowledge, people skills, motivational approach,** and **leading by example.**

Abraham Lincoln, the 16th president of the United States, is also one of the most well-known leaders of all time. He was in office during the American Civil War where he kept the people together and is perhaps the primary reason that the nation held together. He also ended slavery in the United States by signing the Emancipation Proclamation. His greatest characteristics were his **determination, persistence, beliefs,** and **courage.**

Nelson Mandela was the first South African president elected in fully democratic elections. Mandela was also the main player in the anti-apartheid movements in the country and served a lengthy prison sentence because of it. This did not stop Mandela and, in fact, motivated him to devote his life to uniting his country, and he successfully managed to do so after his release from an almost 30-year prison sentence. His main characteristics were his **determination, persistence, focus,** and **will.**

Winston Churchill, Prime Minister of Great Britain from 1940 to 1945, led his country against Nazi Germany during World War II. He teamed up with allies to defeat Hitler. His tenure as the British Prime Minister was in a time of fear and destruction caused by Hitler and his allies. Churchill was known for his **fearlessness, determination, unyielding perseverance,** and **undying devotion to his goal.**

Leadership is not only important on the larger-than-life stage of world history, but also seen day in and day out in companies, agencies, and groups of every size. For that reason, many organizations identify best-practice skills sought in their leaders.

For example, for more than twenty years the U.S. government's Office of Personnel Management (OPM) has used its MOSAIC method (Multi-purpose Occupational Systems Analysis Inventory-Close Ended) to define the tasks and competencies involved in nearly two hundred federal occupations. It views leadership as a competency, i.e., a "measurable pattern of knowledge, skills, abilities, behaviors, and other characteristics that an individual needs to perform work roles or occupational functions successfully."

The term "measurable" in this definition makes it possible to conduct an advanced thought experiment in leadership at a manageable scale. In PerfectCoaches, individuals should be able to assess, on any given day, whether or not they performed that given leadership behavior (i.e., "did" it) every time it was relevant. The discussion to follow describes some leadership competencies identified by OPM. As a thought experiment, you could imagine yourself in a dialog with one outstanding leader asking how well you did.

Research in leadership generally distinguishes between leading tasks, i.e., defining the work and getting it done (sometimes termed "instrumental leadership"), and leading people by motivating other individuals, keeping them working as a team, and keeping them focused (sometimes termed "expressive leadership"). The great leaders are successful in both arenas, and the skillset presented below, which draws largely on the OPM work, makes that distinction.

Leadership

Leading Tasks

- Serve Customers
- Write Effectively
- Solve Problems
- Manage Projects

Leading People

- Work in Teams
- Influence Others
- Communicate Effectively
- Lead Mindfully

Leading Change

- Create and Innovate
- Be Flexible and Adaptable

Leading Tasks

Serve Customers

> *"Earn your success based on service to others, not at the expense of others." – H. Jackson Brown, Jr.*

It is often true that the great leaders on the world stage begin by defining the problem a certain way, then they change the thinking of those they lead. By contrast, the most important task of leaders in business is to serve customers.

Business leaders, particularly entrepreneurs, must first and foremost maintain a customer focus for themselves and their teams and organizations, leading by example. Effective leaders work with clients and customers (that is, any individuals who use or receive the services or products that a work unit produces) to assess their needs, provide information or assistance, resolve their problems, and satisfy their expectations.

As part of their organizational knowledge, they know about available products and services, and are committed to delivering the highest quality results possible, given the situation. A coach might offer feedback by asking: *Did you lead every encounter with a customer so that the result was quality service? Yes, or No? If yes, why were you successful? If no, why not?*

Solve Problems

> *"A problem is a chance for you to do your best."*
> *– Duke Ellington*

Serving customers, be they external paying customers or internal stakeholders (people inside the organization who use a product or service), requires a leader to identify and solve problems. Problem-solving involves gathering information from as many sources as possible, determining the accuracy and relevance of the information, and using sound judgment to create and evaluate alternative solutions.

Once a solution is selected, a recommendation is made, and the solution is implemented.

Solving problems involves the very first skill discussed in this book, which is to fully engage one's brain. Indeed, a feedback question might be: Did you engage your brain today, i.e., did you apply your best thinking to each problem at hand? Yes, or no? If yes, why were you successful? If no, why not? Why does this leadership role pose specific barriers to engaging your brain?

They must propose and then implement new ways to approach each problem. An effective leader develops new insights into situations, questions conventional approaches, and encourages new ideas and innovations.

This often results in leading the team to design and implement new or cutting-edge programs/processes, to be discussed next. A good way to make creativity a habit is to come up with one new idea every day, not necessarily to adopt every idea, but rather to think like an innovator. A coach might offer feedback by asking: *Did you encourage one new idea today? Yes, or No? If yes, why were you successful? If no, why not?*

Manage Projects

> *"Management is doing things right; leadership is doing the right things." – Peter F. Drucker*

Innovative solutions to customer problems often result in the creating of a project—an individual or collaborative enterprise that is carefully planned and designed to achieve a particular aim. There are very specific principles, methods, and tools for project and program management, such as those offered by the Project Management Institute as part of its Project Management Professional (PMP) certification.

Leaders must understand and follow these principles to delegate tasks effectively. The leadership skill of delegation is crucial for successful project management because there is simply too much for one person to do. The book *Change Agents in Sunglasses: The Art and Science of Leadership in the Information Age* describes how a leader must create change agents throughout the organization when large change projects are undertaken.

Leaders must sustain focus even when other people on their team, who may be certified project management professionals, are doing the nuts-and-bolts work of developing, coordinating, and managing resources. Feedback questions concerning project management might include the following: *Did you plan activities and complete deliverables on time today? Yes, or no? If yes, why were you successful? If no, why not?*

Leading People

Write Effectively

> *"Reading maketh a full man; conference a ready man; and writing an exact man." – Francis Bacon*

Writing for pleasure was discussed earlier as an important habit for professional success. It not only stimulates the imagination, but it also provides practice in translating ideas into words.

Francis Bacon, quoted above, was an English philosopher, scientist, and statesman. He is often credited with establishing the importance of empiricism, emphasizing the importance of fact-finding to understanding.

To bring his quotation into a modern leadership context, consider a hypothetical problem-solving situation. The leader reads reports, emails, and other communications to understand the problem. In meetings, he or she confers with others, the goal being to sharpen the team's understanding of the problem and identify alternative solutions. Finally, with as much precision as possible, the "exact" man or woman writes down the solution, using their own words.

In the OPM framework, a leader "recognizes or uses correct English grammar, punctuation, and spelling; communicates information in a succinct and organized manner; produces written information, which may include technical material, that is appropriate for the intended audience." Most leaders have to write one or more things each day. A feedback question would be: *Did you write effectively today? Yes, or no? If yes, why were you successful? If no, why not? Was there something about the situation or topic, or do you need to brush up on your skills?*

Work in Teams

> *"Talent wins games, but teamwork and intelligence*
> *wins championships." – Michael Jordan*

Teamwork often takes individual performance to the next level, and this is especially true in leadership situations. No matter how large the group, two people or two hundred or two hundred million, humans are social creatures who usually accomplish more by working as a team. As discussed earlier, teams are an important concept in PerfectCoaches because they enhance both personal life and professional life. Strong leaders build teams by bringing people together and helping them understand their shared goals and clearly defining their expectations of one another.

Teams come in many sizes ranging from two or three colleagues working in the same office suite to large virtual groups working on a particular project. These large groups can also function well as a team, whether or not they interact face-to-face.

In order to turn a group into a true team, the leader encourages and facilitates cooperation, pride, trust, commitment, team spirit, and group identity. Feedback questions might include the following. *Did you get things done with others today? Yes, or no? If yes, why were you successful? If no, why not?*

Influence Others

> *"The key to successful leadership today is influence,*
> *not authority." – Ken Blanchard*

To lead is to serve customers, solve problems, and manage projects. But there is much more to leadership. Leaders must lead people. Many of the habits and skills discussed elsewhere in the book, such as using social intelligence, are relevant here.

A strong leader moves people forward, persuades others to accept recommendations, cooperate, or change their behavior. That is the measure of influence, culminating, through negotiation and other means, in finding mutually acceptable solutions. The coach might offer feedback by asking these questions: *Did you persuade others to accept recommendations today? Yes, or No? If yes, why were you successful? If no, why not?*

Communicate Effectively

> *"The art of communication is the language*
> *of leadership." – James Humes*

Whole books have been dedicated to effective communication, and many of these focus on how leaders communicate. A leader expresses information (for example, ideas or facts) to individuals or groups effectively. The messages can be complex or simple, depending on the subject, the audience, and the purpose of the communication: Is the topic technical, sensitive, controversial?

Writing is important but speaking to groups can be even more important. Successful leaders make clear and convincing oral presentations. Further, they tune in to the audience, listening to others, noticing nonverbal cues, and responding appropriately. These fundamental skills, discussed elsewhere in the book, are the stock and trade of effective leaders. Feedback questions might include: *Did you see the other person's point of view and get your message across every time today? Yes, or no? If yes, why were you successful? If no, why not?*

Leading Change

Be Flexible and Adaptable

> *"It is not the strongest of the species that survives,*
> *nor the most intelligent. It is the one that is most*
> *adaptable to change." – Charles Darwin*

In the competitive world of business, companies must adapt to changing requirements or perish at the hands of competitors who are better able to adapt. In dynamic, changing circumstances, many of the problems leaders are called upon to solve are ambiguous, i.e., the exact nature of the problem and the source of it are unclear. Leaders must effectively deal with ambiguity, uncertainty, and risks.

A strong leader is always open to change and new information, adapting behavior or work methods in response to new information, changing conditions, or unexpected obstacles. The coach might offer feedback by asking: *Did you adapt your methods to the particulars of the situation? Yes, or No? If yes, why were you successful? If no, why not?*

Create and Innovate

> *"Innovation distinguishes between a leader and a follower." – Steve Jobs*

Creativity and innovation are the hallmarks of great civilizations, great companies, and great leaders. People like Steve Jobs, Thomas Edison, Mary Kay Ash and Walt Disney built thriving companies producing products that changed the world. They were examples of entrepreneurship at its finest.

Entrepreneurs are a special breed of leader, who lead companies they founded and built. Even in organizations where innovation is not a goal in its own right, leaders are required to innovate as they adapt to new situations. Entrepreneurs lead tasks and lead people, as every leader does. However, their special contribution is leading change. They don't simply lead their companies, they create new products that change entire markets and in some cases change the world.

In her book *See, Do, Repeat*, Dr. Rebecca White describes the practice of entrepreneurship. Adaptation, creativity and innovation, the skills required to lead change, are important elements of the entrepreneurial practice.

Interestingly, White links innovation to another important skill of a leader, understanding customers. In her book she tells how she has students of the entrepreneurial practice "create an archetype of their first customer. This is the customer that is going to be the first to adopt and purchase their product. The person who is ready and willing to purchase the product or service to address a need that is not being met. During this process, it is important to visualize the customer, give them a name and a visual appearance, address how they live, and even outline a day in the life of the customer." The ability to understand customers at this level of detail serves leaders in every aspect of their role.

Lead Mindfully

> *"Mindful leadership means seeing the whole situation, within the broadest vista of your own self-awareness."*
> *– Anonymous*

According to OPM guidelines, a successful leader "manages self", i.e., "sets well-defined and realistic personal goals; displays a high level of initiative, effort, and commitment toward completing assignments in a timely manner; works with minimal supervision; is motivated to achieve; demonstrates responsible behavior; assesses and recognizes own strengths and weaknesses; pursues self-development."

Given the importance of mindfulness and self-awareness in PerfectCoaches, these personal characteristics reflect a self-awareness that sets the stage for mindful leadership, the capacity to grasp a situation holistically to include the people, the problem, and the goals.

Perhaps more importantly, mindful leadership involves a personal commitment to motivate others to accomplish a common goal. Our everyday experience and numerous surveys show that leadership skills are highly valued. Many, perhaps most, people are called upon to lead at some time or another.

Within PerfectCoaches, the skillset for leadership rests on other more fundamental skills and habits. For example, delegation is a key leadership skill, so ask yourself if your to-do list includes delegating tasks to others. Leaders usually understand the point of view of others, and that is a general best-practice.

Focused awareness of self, the views of others, and the precise nature of the situation improves leadership. Whether you, make a suggestion, delegate a task, or set the pace for activity, be mindful of how you help define a goal that the group then accomplishes.

One overall theme that the biographies of all great leader's stress is the value of simply staying focused on the ultimate goal, to lead and influence the thoughts and actions of others. Feedback questions may be: *Did you see the whole situation each time you made a decision today? If yes, why were you successful? If no, why not? What can you learn to improve your mindful leadership in situations like the one you encountered?*

So, it would be possible to immerse oneself in the lives of specific leaders or others, and imagine having a dialog with them, even to the point that they work with you on your leadership skills in everyday situations. You could do a similar thought experiment to identify habits for "greatness in everyday life."

Is such a thing possible? We can do advanced thought experiments to assess the possibility. Let's consider four very different writers who provided insight concerning how to live our everyday lives:

- Dale Carnegie, an American lecturer, and writer, popular in the first part of the 20th Century;
- Stephen Covey, also an American, popular toward the end of the 20th Century;
- Viktor Frankel, a psychoanalyst and Holocaust survivor, and
- Rumi, a 13th-century Muslim mystic.

Dale Carnegie

Imagine working with Dale Carnegie, one of the leading twentieth century figures in personal development at both the individual and corporate levels. His advice on working, learning, and living life is timeless and encompasses self-improvement, persuasion, salesmanship, and interpersonal skills. His courses were famous and are still offered today.

Suppose he was helping you build a "Dale Carnegie skillset" by reading your journal, constantly asking questions that would remind you of the principles he set forth in his book *How to Win Friends and Influence People.* He might ask you if you had considered these suggestions for how to win people to your way of thinking:

- *The only way to get the best of an argument is to avoid it.*
- *Show respect for the other person's opinions. Never say, "You're wrong."*
- *If you are wrong, admit it quickly and emphatically.*
- *Begin in a friendly way.*
- *Get the other person saying "yes, yes" immediately.*
- *Let the other person do a great deal of the talking.*
- *Let the other person feel that the idea is his or hers.*
- *Try honestly to see things from the other person's point of view.*
- *Be sympathetic with the other person's ideas and desires.*
- *Appeal to the nobler motives.*
- *Dramatize your ideas.*
- *Throw down a challenge.*

In a similar way, you could use an inner dialog to master not just specific habits suggested in books, videos, and other sources, but rather entire, holistic approaches like the one offered by Dale Carnegie.

Stephen R. Covey

Another comprehensive approach would be to master Stephen R. Covey's "seven habits of highly effective people" as discussed in the highly acclaimed book by that title.

You could begin by going down the list one at a time, saying "Got It!" in your journal after you mastered each one. You would be building a "Stephen Covey habit" that would eventually include all seven habits. The habits, with some commentary in parenthesis to show their relationship to habits discussed earlier, are:

- *Be proactive (you design your own life, so make a habit of taking responsibility for it).*
- *Begin with the end in mind (as in the PerfectCoaches question "Where am I going?" and the best-practice "do each thing for a reason").*
- *Put first things first (do what is both important and urgent first).*
- *Think win-win (i.e., pursue outcomes that benefit everybody).*
- *Seek first to understand, then to be understood (listen mindfully and empathetically, as discussed earlier).*

- *Synergize (bring multiple ideas and forces together).*
- *Sharpen the saw (i.e., continuously improve mind, body, and spirit, as advocated in the PerfectCoaches "healthy living" best practices).*

Like Dale Carnegie, Stephen Covey built an industry around a core set of best practices, and the thought experiment of maintaining a dialog with either of them could be based on their simple success formulas.

Viktor Frankel

For a more complex journey, consider two writers from two unique times of human history and different points of view: Viktor Frankl, a survivor of the 20th-century Holocaust and author of *Man's Search for Meaning,* and Rumi, the 13th-century Islamic philosopher. First, we will look at Frankel's approach.

Viktor Frankel lived through and observed firsthand what was arguably the cruelest institution ever created by man, the Holocaust. Unlike the person-on-person barbarism of the Islamic State of more recent history, the Holocaust fully embraced 20th-century concepts of mass production for the mass-extermination of millions.

Frankel, a Jewish physician, was a survivor of the concentration camps. He observed that those who survived the Holocaust and its concentration camps tended to believe they could still do something important with their lives. They had hope and a vision for life outside of the boundaries of their current condition. Contemplation of the future helped move them beyond the present. These survivors believed that their lives once did, and still could, have meaning. To quote Frankel:

> *Man's search for meaning is the primary motivation of life... This meaning is unique and specific in that it must and will be satisfied by him alone; only then does it achieve a significance which will satisfy his own will to meaning.*

The essence of Frankel's viewpoint is that freedom, in many respects, belongs to an individual.

> *Everything can be taken from a man but one thing: the last of the human freedoms—to choose one's attitude in any given set of circumstances, to choose one's own way.*

Rumi

The concept that freedom is a habit of thought can also be seen in the poetry of Jalal ad-Din Muhammad Balch-Rumi, better known today as Rumi.

Rumi was a Muslim theologian and mystic. Although his work has become popular in the United States in recent years, he is perhaps best known for the dance of the Whirling Dervishes, a physical statement of moving toward "the perfect". According to the story, one day as he walked through a city, he was overtaken by joy. The inner experience of joy was so strong that it moved him to spread his arms and begin spinning in circles, whirling. This became the groundwork for the dance and related Sufi meditation form that is practiced today.

Rumi poems contain what can be thought of as a mystical tolerance of diverse beliefs. Rumi's writings also emphasize the importance of connecting oneself with the world and understanding the consequences of both thought and action. In *If Though Wilt Be Observant*, he says:

> *If thou wilt be observant and vigilant, thou wilt see at every moment the response to thy action. Be observant if thou wouldst have a pure heart, for something is born to thee in consequence of every action.*

Rumi also knew the importance of having a vision that keeps us moving forward. His poem *One Who Wraps Himself* reads:

> *Constant, slow movement teaches us to keep working,*
> *Like a small creek that stays clear,*
> *That doesn't stagnate, but finds a way*
> *Through numerous details, deliberately.*

As writers, Frankl and Rumi drew on deep convictions about what human life means and, more importantly, what the world is truly about. Even the most advanced thought experiment involving Viktor Frankl or Rumi need not be mystical or complicated. On the other hand, an imagined conversation with them could be very informative and span the entire realm of philosophy.

What is morally right? What is beauty? What is the basis of knowledge? What is the nature of reality? Imagined conversations with Viktor Frankel or Rumi could breath life into these thorny issues of ethics, aesthetics, epistemology, and metaphysics.

Yet it is also true that both thinkers can provide useful feedback to you about how to live each day fully and mindfully. In fact, an imagined conversation with any of the leaders and thinkers discussed in this book can be a useful exercise. As Rumi says, your journey "stays clear" by constantly moving forward, "finding a way through numerous details, deliberately."

Summing Up
Making the PerfectCoaches
work for You

The Greatest Salesman in the World, like Dale Carnegie's *How to Win Friends and Influence People,* offers ideas that apply to everyone. In addition, habits like "always be confident" and "always be charming" are not only the best practices for persuasion, but they can also bring success and satisfaction to every aspect of life. When we see how such diverse roles as leadership, sales, and customer service can apply the PerfectCoaches method, the power of its discipline and simplicity becomes apparent.

PerfectCoaches is, in fact, nothing more nor less than a simple, straightforward thought experiment. It poses fundamental questions about who you are, what you do, and where you want to go, then *invites* you to imagine "perfect coaches" asking the questions in what can be an enjoyable, lifelong Socratic dialog.

The PerfectCoaches method also *challenges* you to become the person you want to be, one small change at a time. This To-Be self is likely to contain the best practices suggested in this book as well as other habits you want to master. The app itself provides a slightly different list of behaviors.

https://users.perfectcoaches.com/home/how_do_i_change

The app also contains learning modules for each of the foundational best practice behaviors. Click the lightbulb to see the additional information.

The virtual coach interacting with users in the PerfectCoaches app is perfectly patient, disciplined, committed to simplicity, and ready to accept you as you are today. For a better understanding of AMI, the computer-based virtual coach, go to this URL:

https://www.youtube.com/watch?v=NoBzkz0G5EU

The PerfectCoaches process works because you make it work. At the foundation are brief journal entries that keep you focused on the best-practice habit you are trying to learn and the ones you have already mastered.

The role of the virtual coach is simply to reinforce that focus. The coach interacting with you and your diary entries may be a person you know, or someone you have never met. In advanced thought experiments, you can imagine someone from history or pop culture playing that role. The identity of your coach is less important than your capacity to think about the questions they ask as feedback to your journal entries.

With a professional coach, there are certain characteristics that make them fantastic at their job and a positive influence on you. These characteristics are part of the PerfectCoaches method, and should be kept in mind as you work the questions and become more self-aware. The virtual coach is meant to be:

- Perfectly patient
- Perfectly focused on the future
- Perfectly committed to simplicity
- Perfectly disciplined
- Perfectly at ease with the human condition

When you are employing PerfectCoaches in your own life, you are in your own thoughts. As the biggest and most important team player on your team, you should keep these characteristics in mind whenever you feel like you are struggling. Give yourself some grace and compassion, because, as Mother Teresa said, life is a struggle. Knowing how struggle and sadness are part of life, let yourself "Do Happy" whenever you can.

In the end, the process belongs to you *as you work and learn in teams*. It invites you to imagine what your groups, no matter what the size, would be like if everybody did as well, and felt as well, as they could. Going beyond specific best practices, PerfectCoaches prepares you to change not only yourself but the world around you. The first step is understanding your core self: the roles you play, your behavior, and your inner experiences.

Self-awareness is a gift that comes with being human. It is a source of joy and power. Take advantage of it. Savor it. Each of us has the chance to cultivate it to find meaning in life, connect to the world and people around us, and live each moment mindfully and holistically.

Glossary of Terms

Activity: something that you do, usually involving a plan.

As-Is State: in Business Process Reengineering (BPR), the way a system works right now.

Behavior: the actions by which an organism adjusts to its environment (*American Psychological Association's Glossary of Terms*), used in PerfectCoaches as the all-encompassing term for habits, skills, activities, and inner experiences.

Behavioral Focus: a type of mindfulness that enables you to understand the cues (antecedent events) and reinforcement (consequences) that determine the likelihood that a target behavior will be performed in a given situation.

Best-Practice: in Business Process Reengineering (BPR), a method or process that should be adopted because it has proven to be successful when used by others.

Business Process Reengineering (BPR): a set of process analysis and improvement techniques designed to move a business from a flawed "As-Is" state to a preferred "To-Be" vision.

(The) Coaches: in the PerfectCoaches thought experiment, a proper noun referring specifically to questions imagined as people asking the questions.

Coaching Culture: an organizational commitment to guiding individual development in everything from performance assessments to training programs.

Cue: used synonymously with the concept of a "trigger", an event (antecedent stimulus) that causes a person to behave in a certain way.

Core Self: the animating force in your day-to-day life, revealed in who you are and what you do and consisting of roles, behaviors, and inner experiences.

Doctrine of the Four Ts: the principle that people often work best in teams, and teams perform best when *talking*, *training*, and *thanking* are encouraged inside of the team.

Emotional Intelligence: in PerfectCoaches, a by-product of self-awareness that improves the performance of persuasion professionals by enabling them to understand, label, and manage their inner experiences as well as the inner experiences of others.

Feedback: the effect of some action being "fed-back" to the system so as to influence the next thing the system does, used in PerfectCoaches as a way to reinforce behavioral focus.

Habits: behaviors performed repetitively in situations, with cues in the environment stimulating behavior which may then be reinforced positively (making it more likely to occur the next time the stimulus is presented) or negatively (making it less likely to occur).

High-Level Wellness: an integrated approach to health that emphasizes the connection between nutrition, exercise, and a positive attitude toward living.

Inner Accountant: in the PerfectCoaches thought experiment, the Coach constantly asking "Why are you doing that? Have you really considered the costs and awards associated with each thing you do?"

Inner Craftsman: in the PerfectCoaches thought experiment, the Coach constantly asking "Have you practiced your craft with pride? Have you done your best work?"

Inner Experience: things you are feeling and thoughts you are having inside, although they can sometimes manifest themselves in behavior seen by others, such as in facial expressions.

Inner Planner: in the PerfectCoaches thought experiment, the Coach emphasizing the value of having a vision of your future self.

Journal: a personal record of events and how the writer reacts to them, used in PerfectCoaches to not only record events, but to help the virtual coach sustain focus on changes to habits, skills, and other behaviors.

Kaizen Events: derived from a Japanese word for the practice of continuous improvement ("good change") in business, typically workshops where problems are identified, and corrective actions are proposed; it is possible for an organization to consider the Journal as a "24x7 virtual Kaizen event."

Knowledge Workers: workers whose main capital is knowledge and thinking for a living, including software engineers, physicians, architects, engineers, scientists, lawyers, academics, and students, who are apprentice knowledge workers.

Life's 7 Perfect Coaches: personifications of life's fundamental questions: *Who am I? What do I do? Why do I do it? When do I do it best? Where do I want to go in life? How do I change? What if I could change the world?* The coaches are the questions, and the questions are the coaches.

Motivational Interviewing: first discussed by William R. Miller and Stephen Rollnick as a psychotherapeutic technique but later applied to many types of personal development, motivational interviewing is a dialog designed to foster positive decisions and goal attainment, typically involving small changes.

Mindfulness: a clear, purposefulness awareness of the events taking place right now, in the present moment; the capacity to focus on oneself, the views of others, and the precise nature of the situation.

Persuasion Professional: professionals in sales, leadership, management, and customer service for whom influencing the thoughts and actions of others is a core competency.

Reinforcement: a consequence of behavior that will make the behavior more or less likely to be performed again.

Role: a way to group a set of specific behaviors associated with a category of person, e.g., student, nurse, salesperson, mother, father, brother, sister, manager, etc.

(The) Sam Walton Imperative: measuring the effectiveness of leadership and customer service based on customer retention, reflecting the quote, attributed to Sam Walton, that "There is only one boss. The customer. And he can fire everybody in the company from the chairman on down, simply by spending his money somewhere else."

(The) Science of Pure Performance: an organizational development methodology enabling leaders to focus on measuring results; fostering change and continuous improvement; and achieving the most with people, often the most important and challenging component of a people-process-technology system.

Self-Awareness: the capacity to reflect upon one's own behavior, setting the stage for understanding who you are today and envisioning who you could be tomorrow.

Skillset: a list of foundational behaviors that are learned individually but practiced together to achieve a single goal, displayed in the PerfectCoaches app as "Got It!" behaviors you have mastered and continue to use each time it is appropriate to do so.

Skillset Résumé: a summary of core skills, a way to communicate the business value of a skills acquired by using Perfect Coaches.

Socratic Dialog: a method of critical thinking attributed to the Greek philosopher Socrates in which insight is gained by continuously asking questions, used in PerfectCoaches to guide the dialog with the virtual coach.

Target Behavior: a habit or skill identified as a target for acquisition or change.

Thought Experiments: devices of the imagination used to investigate the nature of things (*Stanford Encyclopedia of Philosophy*), employed in PerfectCoaches to investigate the nature of the self by imagining questions as if they were coaches.

To-Be State: in Business Process Reengineering (BPR), one or more ways to implement improved processes in the future.

To-Eat List: a special to-do list consisting of a simple daily plan for what you will eat and drink, plus when and where you will have your meals and snacks.

Trial Close: a key part of persuasion in which you assess the customer's readiness to buy by asking for an opinion about your product while using emotional intelligence to pay attention to the customer's body language and facial expressions, not just their words.

Virtual Coach: the coach who conducts the online motivational interview and provides feedback to journal entries in the form of a brief question in order to sustain mindfulness and improve the probability that another journal entry will be made.

Appendix 1

A "Pen and Paper" Workbook

This workbook is an alternative to using the PerfectCoaches app. You can write your "selfie in words", recording who you are and who you want to be. It also provides space for thirty days of short journal entries. This mirrors thirty days using the PerfectCoaches app and reflects the observation that daily journal entries can help people learn three new habits in thirty days (the "3-in-30 goal").

Answer the question *Who am I?* with the first thoughts that come to mind.

Who Am I?

_____

_____

_____

_____

_____

_____

_____

You are what you repeatedly do. In the spaces below, answer *What are the five most important things I do? Why do I do it?* And *When do I do it best?*

	What do I do?	**Why do I do it?**	**When do I do it best?**
1			
2			
3			
4			
5			

Where am I going? Answer the question with the first thoughts that come to mind.

_____

_____

_____

_____

_____

_____

_____

_____

_____

_____

_____

_____

_____

_____

_____

_____

How do I change? Answer for at least one, but no more than three, behaviors.

Activities or Habits to Start, Stop, or Improve	Method
FIRST:	___ IMITATE another person as a model ___ SUBSTITUTE one behavior for another ___ CHANGE SCRIPT for a role you play ___ INCREASE MINDFULNESS of why you do it ___ TRAIN to do new behavior(s)
SECOND:	___ IMITATE another person as a model ___ SUBSTITUTE one behavior for another ___ CHANGE SCRIPT for a role you play ___ INCREASE MINDFULNESS of why you do it ___ TRAIN to do new behavior(s)
THIRD:	___ IMITATE another person as a model ___ SUBSTITUTE one behavior for another ___ CHANGE SCRIPT for a role you play ___ INCREASE MINDFULNESS of why you do it ___ TRAIN to do new behavior(s)

My Journal

Day 1:

_____

_____

_____

Day 2:

_____

_____

_____

Day 3:

_____

_____

_____

Day 4:

_____

_____

_____

Day 5:

_____

_____

_____

Day 6:

_____

_____

_____

Day 7:

_____

_____

_____

Day 8:

_____

_____

_____

Day 9:

_____

_____

_____

Day 10:

_____

_____

_____

Day 11:

_____

_____

_____

Day 12:

_____

_____

_____

Day 13:

_____

_____

_____

Day 14:

_____

_____

_____

Day 15:

_____

_____

_____

Day 16:

_____

_____

_____

Day 17:

_____

_____

_____

Day 18:

_____

_____

_____

Day 19:

_____

_____

_____

Day 20:

_____

_____

_____

Day 21:

_____

_____

_____

Day 22:

_____

_____

_____

Day 23:

_____

_____

_____

Day 24:

_____

_____

_____

Day 25:

_____

_____

_____

Day 26:

_____

_____

_____

Day 27:

_____

_____

_____

Day 28:

_____

_____

_____

Day 29:

_____

_____

_____

Day 30:

_____

_____

_____

Appendix 2

Sample To-Do and To-Eat Lists

To-Do List for Today

>   Make sure rent check cleared
>   Call Roger RE next weekend
>   Finish the write-up on next steps
>   Confirm appointments for the week of the 10th
>   Get another car insurance quote

To-Do List for Today

>   Finish cleaning the house
>   Get to soccer practice early
>   Return books to library

My To-Eat List for Today

>   Cereal for breakfast with coffee and orange juice
>   (about 300 calories)
>   Granola bar around 11 AM (130 calories)
>   Lunch, probably McDonalds on the road around 1 PM;
>   Big Mac meal 950 calories
>   Protein drink – 150 calories, around 3 PM
>   Dinner at home 7 PM—salad, salmon, baked potato
>   (700 calories)
>   2 glasses of wine (150 calories each)
>
>   Light workout at the gym 5 PM
>   Total 2200 calories – 200 over the 2,000-calorie goal

My To-Eat List for Today with "banana equivalents"

Cereal for breakfast with coffee and orange juice (about 300 calories, 3 bananas worth of calories)

Granola bar around 11 AM (130 calories, 1 banana)

Lunch probably McDonalds on the road 1 PM – big Mac meal 950 calories, 10 bananas

Protein drink – 150 calories, around 3 PM, 1 banana

Dinner at home 7 PM—salad, salmon, baked potato probably 700 calories, let's say 7 bananas worth

2 glasses of wine,150 calories each, 3 bananas

Light workout at the gym 5 PM

Total 24 bananas – over by 400 calories

About the Author

V. Douglas Hines, Ph.D., is the founder of The VARI (Virtual Applied Research International) Group and creator of the organizational development method *The Science of Pure Performance.*® The human resources component of the method is separately branded as *PerfectCoaches.*®

Dr. Hines began his scientific career as a research assistant in the neuroscience laboratory of what was then known as Friends of Psychiatric Research. He earned his Ph.D. in applied social psychology at the University of Maryland. He is a member Emeritus of the American Association for the Advancement of Science, the author of two college textbooks and several business books and has taught at the Robert H. Smith School of Business and the Institute for Systems Research at the University of Maryland. He also served as Director of Maryland's Open University program.

A former Principal/Partner at KPMG, much of his professional life has been devoted on the applied arts of consulting and business process reengineering. Having helped many organizations move from a flawed "as-is" state to a preferred "to-be" vision, he believes the same disciplined process can help people achieve the individual excellence that is not only rewarding for them but fosters quality and improved performance for their enterprise.

Consulting and university teaching have also convinced him that, to get the right *answers*, you must ask the right *questions*. The *PerfectCoaches* logo, a perfect sphere rising above its own image, symbolizes how continuous improvement requires self-reflection. This book is about asking the questions, and finding the answers, that will improve the performance of students, professionals, and everyone who wants to enjoy a complete and healthy life.

www.ingramcontent.com/pod-product-compliance
Lightning Source LLC
Chambersburg PA
CBHW071235210326
41597CB00016B/2060